SPECTACULAR WINERIES
of Sonoma County

A CAPTIVATING TOUR OF ESTABLISHED, ESTATE AND BOUTIQUE WINERIES

Published by

Panache Partners, LLC
1424 Gables Court
Plano, TX 75075
469.246.6060
Fax: 469.246.6062
www.panache.com

Publishers: Brian G. Carabet and John A. Shand

Principal photographer: M.J. Wickham

Printed in Malaysia

Distributed by Independent Publishers Group
800.888.4741

PUBLISHER'S DATA

Spectacular Wineries of Sonoma County

Library of Congress Control Number: 2009928582

ISBN 13: 978-1-933415-66-6
ISBN 10: 1-933415-66-5

First Printing 2010

10 9 8 7 6 5 4 3 2 1

Right: Stonestreet Winery, page 258
Previous Page: Jacuzzi Family Vineyards, page 130

Panache Partners, LLC, is dedicated to the restoration and conservation of
the environment. Our *Spectacular Wineries* books are manufactured with
strict adherence to an environmental management system in accordance
with ISO 14001 standards, including the use of paper from mills certified
to derive their products from well-managed forests. We are committed to
continued investigation of alternative paper products and environmentally
responsible manufacturing processes to ensure the preservation of our
fragile planet.

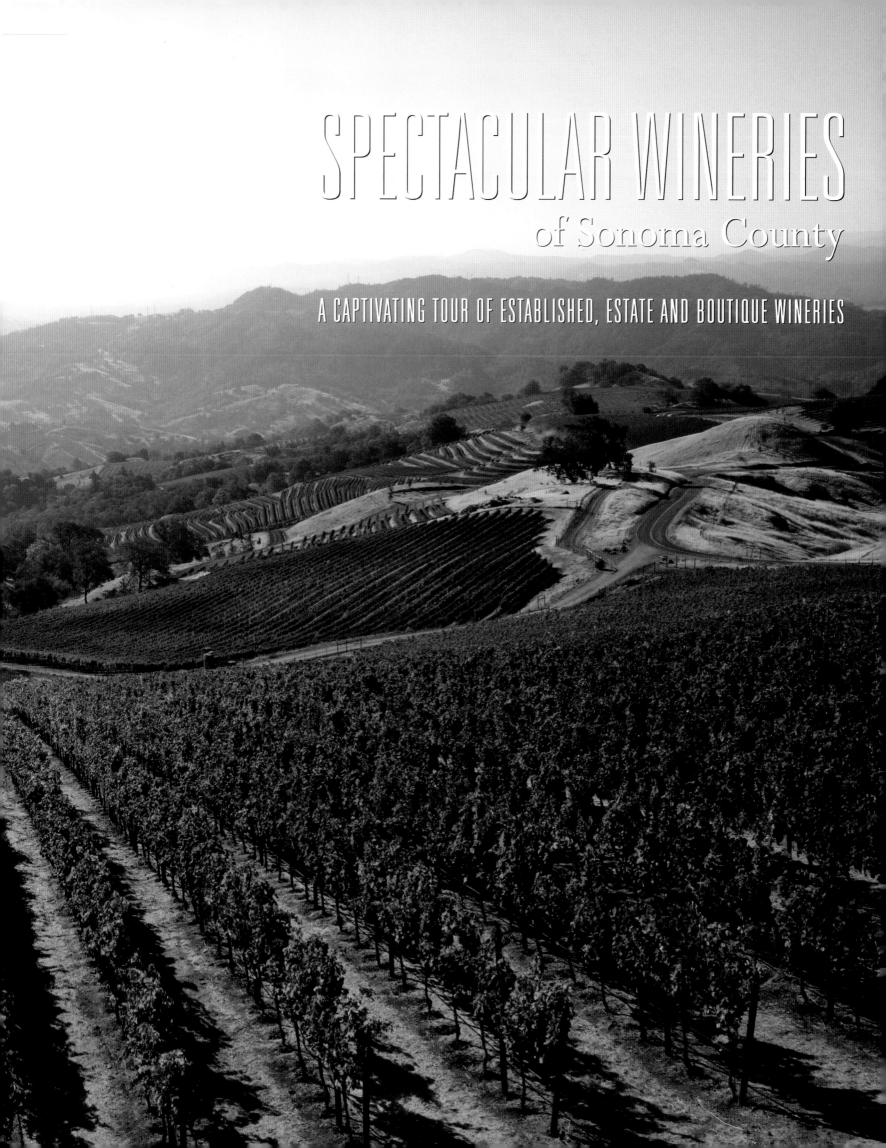

SPECTACULAR WINERIES
of Sonoma County

A CAPTIVATING TOUR OF ESTABLISHED, ESTATE AND BOUTIQUE WINERIES

MacMurray Ranch, page 178

4

Introduction

When we talk of California's wine country, inevitable regional comparisons seem to pop up. Why? Because we all want to come here, and there's not enough time in the world to capture it all. So, we narrow the focus. Among California's varied regions you can find some of the world's most remarkable wines over a terrain that offers such beautiful vistas that you start to wonder if it's possible to go back to Eden.

Among these regions, Sonoma County literally has a huge advantage; the county is bigger, wider and therefore more diverse. Over 200,000 acres in size, some 250 wineries call Sonoma County home. It was here that pinot noir and zinfandel took root—and wine drinkers across the world quickly took notice. Here, you will also find other excellent varietals, including chardonnay, sauvignon blanc, pinot blanc, pinot gris, cabernet sauvignon, merlot, syrah, cabernet franc, sangiovese and petite sirah. This is a wonderland for the intimate tasting experience with the winemaker, vintner and the family.

Since I started coming out to wine country, Sonoma County has mesmerized me. Not only is the wine fantastic, but the land itself is heaven. I'd be surprised if anyone came and didn't think, "You know, I could live out here." Healdsburg, for example, has always drawn my attention. This is one of those towns where you can just sit in the square, drinking a cup of coffee, and try not to fall out of your chair thinking about how wonderful your next few meals are going to be.

With *Spectacular Wineries of Sonoma County*, I want to take you through this gorgeous place, for the experience is unparalleled. This varied collection of wineries celebrates the art of winemaking, as well as the art, architecture, culture, heritage and way of life that for centuries has graced the region. I want you to experience the viticultural areas, such as Alexander, Russian River, Dry Creek and Sonoma valleys. Here, you'll be introduced to such players as Audelssa Estate Winery, Cline Cellars, Iron Horse Vineyards, Jordan and J. Rochioli. You'll also meet the Rafanellis, the Robledos and many others. This book is about good wine and good people. And, of course, the good Earth.

Each winery produces outstanding and often award-winning wine while offering gracious hospitality and sharing their immense passion. Sit back and enjoy a glass of your favorite wine for this journey through Sonoma County.

Cheers,

Kathryn Newell

Regional Publisher

Photograph by M.J. Wickham

Contents

Sonoma County

Kendall-Jackson Vineyard Estates, page 146

Behind the Wines

"Life in Sonoma County is very much about vines, vintages and variety. You feel it everywhere when you are here; as you drive around you cannot help but notice the changes in the vineyards as the vintage progresses; in the restaurants you see the local vintners with their wines, you see artisan producers of cheeses, produce, mushrooms, lamb, you even see the fish mongers with oysters, crab and salmon. It is a good life and one we love to share with visitors."

—Juelle Fisher, Fisher Vineyards

"From the unspoiled beauty of the land to its storied history, friendly people, easygoing pace and quality of life, Sonoma is quite simply a world-class destination."

—Bill Brinton, Charles Creek Vineyards

Hartford Family Winery, page 102

Stryker Sonoma Winery, page 264

Lancaster Estate, page 162

Iron Horse Vineyards, page 118

Freeman Vineyard & Winery, page 84

Hanzell Vineyards, page 94

Ledson Winery & Vineyards, page 172

Seghesio Family Vineyards, page 242

Landmark Vineyards, page 168

Robledo Family Winery, page 222

Michel-Schlumberger Wine Estate, page 198

Verité Winery, page 268

Simi Winery, page 246

Keller Estate Winery & Vineyards, page 142

"Once off the vine, it is only a matter of how much of the grape's potential we can capture and how much will slip through our fingers."

—Steven Canter, Quivira Vineyards

"It seems that every moment of every day, somewhere in Sonoma County the light is right for a spectacular photograph. I simply try to stay alert."

—M.J. Wickham, M.J. Wickham Photography

"It is a privilege and great pleasure to live and work in Sonoma County wine country. Every morning, as I walk my dog, I continue to be stunned by the natural beauty ... hot air balloons rising out of the fog, the mountains looming on the horizon, and enjoying another sunny day in the outdoors!"

—Nancy Frey, Ascentia Wine Estates

"To grow grapes and make wine is not a job that you clock in and clock out of—it is a way of life."

—Rashell Rafanelli-Fehlman, A. Rafanelli Winery

Foppiano Vineyards, page 78

deLorimier Vineyards & Winery, page 56

Haywood Estate, page 106

J. Rochioli Vineyard and Winery, page 124

Fisher Vineyards, page 72

Matanzas Creek Winery, page 186

Deerfield Ranch Winery, page 52

Mazzocco Sonoma Winery, page 134

A. Rafanelli Winery, page 18

Jordan Vineyard & Winery, page 134

Ferrari-Carano Vineyards and Winery, page 66

Benziger Family Winery, page 30

"It's a life's work to make wines that are genuinely connected with a place and the people who farm the land."

—Mike Benziger, Benziger Family Winery

"Sonoma is like your favorite walking shoes. It may not have the latest flash but nothing is more comfortable or gets the job done better."

—Charles G. Tsegeletos, Cline Cellars & Jacuzzi Family Vineyards

Lambert Bridge Winery, page 154

Passalacqua Winery, page 206

Sonoma County

A. Rafanelli Winery

Healdsburg

For the Rafanellis, wine is the family business. A four-generation, totally family-run estate, A. Rafanelli Winery has the rare opportunity to practice what many wineries lose over time: quality over quantity. Producing some 11,000 cases annually, the winery sells out of every bottle, often within days of release. The key to the Rafanellis' success is growing great grapes and making great wine in their bucolic spot in the Dry Creek Valley, perpetuating a history of wine craftsmanship.

Alberto Rafanelli found himself in America in 1906. Raised in a disadvantaged family in Tuscany, Alberto sought a new life here, bringing along his wife, Litizia. She was from a winemaking family—bringing instrumental elements to the future winery—but, as things go, her brother stood to inherit the family winery in Italy. So, Alberto and Litizia, wanting a rural lifestyle, moved out to Healdsburg, bought some property with a few small loans, and began the hard yet rewarding work of farming. The wine line continued: first with Americo Rafanelli, who was born in America, who loved farming and who produced only zinfandels, for they were his favorite; second with David Rafanelli, son of Americo and a 60-year veteran of the vineyard lifestyle; and third with Rashell Rafanelli-Fehlman, David's daughter and the winery's current winemaker. A. Rafanelli Winery is truly a family experience.

Top Left: Hand-picked estate grapes in half-ton, stainless bins wait to be delivered to the winery.
Photograph by M.J. Wickham

Bottom Left: Limited production wines produced at the winery—zinfandel, cabernet sauvignon, merlot and Terrace Select—sit in the cave's dining room.
Photograph by M.J. Wickham

Facing Page: The winery's steeply terraced hillside of vertically trained cabernet sauvignon looks out toward Mt. St. Helena.
Photograph by M.J. Wickham

The great thing about wine is that each vintage is a little different. Part of the fun is to taste current and old wines, and with a Rafanelli wine, you are never dealing with an exact duplication; you are always looking at something new. Early in the history of American winemaking, the focus was on bulk wines. The market started to change in the '60s and '70s, birthing the demand for premium wines. This was an exiting time for A. Rafanelli Winery, for it was an opportunity to dedicate to quality. But even now, there is a very distinct, very youthful feel in the industry. "We're really at the birth of winemaking in America," says David.

And Sonoma is the perfect place from which to produce. The most varied of appellations, with more diversity of climate and soil than some other California counties, Sonoma is virgin land, and planting here means that the Rafanellis can be very selective of what and where

they are growing. Typically, about two-thirds of the bottles produced under the A. Rafanelli label are zinfandels, with roughly a third going to cabernets. Throw in a couple hundred cases of merlot and a reserve cabernet—during those years of extremely good grapes—and you have a first-class catalog of fine wines that have branched from the distinctive, all-zinfandel winery of America's days at the helm.

Above: A 100-year-old redwood barn was converted from a workhorse barn to a working winery by Americo Rafanelli of the second generation.
Photograph by M.J. Wickham

Right: Three 1945 Chevrolet grape trucks are full of merlot grapes for delivery. The trucks were originally used to haul grapes to San Francisco by the family in the 1940s.
Photograph by M.J. Wickham

Facing Page Top: One of the winery's head-pruned zinfandel vineyards sits above the Dry Creek Valley floor in early spring.
Photograph courtesy of A. Rafanelli Winery

Facing Page Bottom: The winery is on its third and fourth generation: Craig Fehlman, vineyard manager, Rashell Rafanelli-Fehlman, winemaker, Patty and David Rafanelli, proprietors, and Stacy Rafanelli, production manager, along with the dogs, Bodie and Milo.
Photograph by M.J. Wickham

Above Top: Behind the winery, nestled between the olive orchards and hillside vineyards, is the lake inhabited by numerous frogs, ducks and wild Canadian geese.
Photograph by M.J. Wickham

Above Middle: Numerous roses flank the property at the hillside vineyards and olive orchards. The winery is now harvesting and producing its own estate olive oil.
Photograph by M.J. Wickham

Above Bottom: Family legacy is important. The second-generation Americo Rafanelli and third-generation David Rafanelli pose in the winery.
Photograph courtesy of A. Rafanelli Winery

Left: From the olive orchards, the original farmhouse, built in the early 1920s, overlooks the winery's various Dry Creek Valley vineyard blocks of cabernet, merlot, syrah and chardonnay.
Photograph by M.J. Wickham

While never wanting to be tied to certain varietals, the A. Rafanelli Winery team doesn't like too many changes. It is important for the family to maintain a consistency across the board, manifest the best grapes in the old, traditional method of winemaking. But this is agriculture and, as David says, you have to make what Mother Nature gives you. Maintaining their own hillside vineyards for more concentration, the Rafanellis self-bottle their mountain-grown fruit. This intentional sizing of their volume stemmed from what others might call a gift: publicity. After raves in *The Wall Street Journal* and *The New York Times* exploded the run on Rafanelli wines, the winery found itself overselling, knowing

that quality would be lost in overproduction. Now that they are firmly set upon the map of remarkable Sonoma wineries, they have settled into a comfortable position. With a century of accumulated experience, the family maintains a tradition of producing premium grapes and handcrafting world-class wines.

Above: In the middle of the underground caves, the cabernet sauvignons and merlots are aged; the cave's constant temperature and humidity are energy efficient and ideal for cellaring the premium wines.
Photograph by M.J. Wickham

Facing Page: The redwood-beamed entrance leads to the underground cellars and dining room.
Photograph by M.J. Wickham

To taste a Rafanelli wine, you may have to order from the winery directly—at which you will most certainly come in direct contact with one of the Rafanelli clan—or come across a bottle in one of the key restaurants featuring the label; but the action is more than worth the effort: Your mouth will certainly thank you.

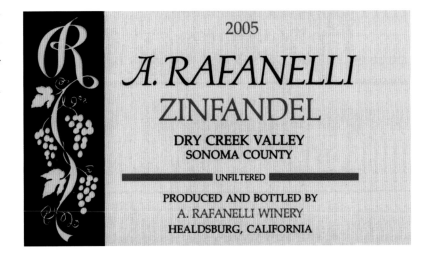

WINE & FARE

Dry Creek Valley Zinfandel

Pair with a pork ragout with porcini mushrooms on a bed of creamy polenta.

Merlot

Pair with risotto and shaved black truffle, or seared rare ahi tuna.

Cabernet Sauvignon

Pair with braised beef short ribs in a reduction sauce, or shaved Sonoma dry jack cheese with roasted red beets and truffle honey.

Tastings
Open by appointment only

Audelssa Estate Winery

Glen Ellen

There is viticulture, and then there is extreme viticulture. Sometimes the most distinguishing element of a vineyard is the intense nature of its site. Audelssa Estate Winery has one of the most distinctive vineyard sites in California. Cascading some 1,200 vertical feet down the Sonoma slope of the Mayacamas Mountains, this fascinating hillside location shows extreme diversity over 80 planted acres. Its southwest-facing perch on the Sonoma side of Mount Veeder provides both an amazing view of San Francisco and wines that are elegant, complex and sophisticated.

Dan and Jeanne Schaefer began to plant vines on this site in 1990 after searching exhaustively for the ideal conditions in which to grow world-class cabernet sauvignon and syrah. During the vineyard's formative years, Audelssa's wines were made by the iconic Richard Arrowood at nearby Arrowood Vineyards & Winery. Arrowood's Erich Bradley thought Audelssa would benefit from producing wines in a more artisanal fashion, enabling them to capture the essence of the terroir. His dream, albeit unorthodox, was to produce Audelssa's Bordeaux and Rhône wines in the Burgundian winemaking tradition in order to create the most graceful and seductive expressions of this special place.

Top Left: After a vineyard tour, visitors can enjoy a picnic lunch and views at the winery. The inside features a dining room, fireplace and comfortable lounge.
Photograph by M.J. Wickham

Middle Left: Everywhere one turns, another scenic vignette reveals itself. Here, the view is down the Sonoma side of Mount Veeder looking toward the valley floor.
Photograph by Jim Taft

Bottom Left: Vibrant green grass brought on by early winter rains in this block of syrah appears to spill into the Bay area with Mount Tamalpais in the distance.
Photograph by Jim Taft

Facing Page: Fog from the Pacific Ocean and San Francisco Bay creeps up to the property, providing a welcome break from the afternoon heat in late autumn.
Photograph by Jim Taft

The second generation of Schaefers, Dan Jr. and Gloria, asked Erich to become Audelssa's winemaker in 2002, and together they examined the complex, hillside vineyards. They noted the two soil types that span the acreage—rhyolite and basalt—and intuitively felt that each must influence the grapes in powerful and unique ways. Immediately after the 2002 harvest, it was evident to all who tasted them that the wines made from the different soils were vastly different. The one thing they shared in common was a smooth, silky texture that is best attributed to the gentle approach taken in the winery.

Top Left: The Schaefer family: Dan Jr. and Gloria Schaefer, Dan Sr. and Jeanne Schaefer and daughters Audrey, Chelsea and Alyssa—from whom the name Audelssa is derived.
Photograph by M.J. Wickham

Middle Left: The wines of Audelssa are a compelling bunch.
Photograph by M.J. Wickham

Bottom Left: Cascading down the mountainside, the severity of the terrain is the secret to producing wines of extraordinary concentration and intensity.
Photograph by Jim Taft

Facing Page: In the distance beyond post-harvest amber vines is Mount Diablo, the Bay Area's second highest peak; the views can easily extend 60 miles or more on clear days.
Photograph by Jim Taft

Audelssa—the name an abridgement of the Schaefer daughters' names—is a winery that truly echoes its circumstances. The dramatic vineyards are inimitable thanks to restrictions on the development of hillside vineyards that went into effect in Sonoma County in 2000. Even the label reveals an image that could either be the extreme elevation or the strong winds that blow intensely over the terrain. These forceful conditions ultimately produce Audelssa wines: a worthy goal of a winery with moxie.

WINE & FARE

Audelssa Zephyr

Pair with chicken liver boudin served on a crostini with pear mostarda and saba.

Audelssa Tempest

Pair with star anise-seared ahi tuna served on a wonton crisp with pickled beet, surrey arugula and beet vinaigrette.

Audelssa Summit

Pair with lamb sliders with harissa aioli served on brioche with pickled red onion and pepper cress.

Audelssa Cabernet Sauvignon Reserve

Pair with chocolate budino topped with Maldon sea salt, pine nuts and Solara extra virgin olive oil.

Tastings
Available at Audelssa Glen Ellen Tasting Room
Open to the public, year-round

Benziger Family Winery

Glen Ellen

Almost 30 years ago, Mike and Mary Benziger left White Plains, New York, and came to Sonoma Valley with the intention of starting their own winery. The branches of the family tree began to cross the United States as Mike's six siblings and parents arrived over the next few years. With a few dozen family members in the vicinity to craft Benziger wine, the family investment was total. These days the winery overflows with Benzigers as the next generation gets ready to enter the business.

The Benzigers focus on wine that expresses individual vineyards, with farming practices that rely on integrity and respect for the land. This effort of holistic agriculture is the driving force behind their namesake brand, while also functioning as a model for high sustainability in the field.

To get at the authenticity of the site and the greatest caliber fruit, Benziger's farming practices exist on a couple of planes. Organics, of course, is the elimination of synthetic chemical assistance to the vineyards. Biodynamics, on the other hand, is the vision of the farm as a whole, encompassing the entire estate, using natural life forces to reach sustainability and self-sufficiency. Benziger also utilizes a method called Farming for Flavors, which is a certified third-party program that requires any of the winery's growers to meet a standard of excellence in promoting healthy environments.

Top Left: A steel gate beckons visitors into Bruno Benziger's—the family patriarch—Nymph Garden located off the front porch of the ranch house on the Benziger estate.
Photograph by M.J. Wickham

Bottom Left: Trellises constructed from barrel stays lie at the entrance of the property's insectaries—land devoted to plants that attract beneficial mites, bugs, butterflies, birds and small animals that prey on pests harmful to grapevines.
Photograph by M.J. Wickham

Facing Page: Walkways dot the Benziger Family Winery, guiding visitors to the gardens, the tasting room and the old ranch house where the family first lived.
Photograph courtesy of Benziger Family Winery

Above: At Benziger, water used in winemaking flows from a collection pond through an embankment of water plants into a lower pond. The root systems of the plants act like a filter and cleanse the water of impurities.
Photograph by M.J. Wickham

Left: While Benziger Family Winery is off the beaten path, the trip is worth the effort. Visitors can stroll through the Biodynamic Discovery Trail, take one of two tours, visit the tasting room, have a picnic and much, much more.
Photograph by M.J. Wickham

Above: The goal with Benziger's Biodynamic estate is to energize and enhance the incredible environment that surrounds the grapes. With this in mind, the Benzigers are as attentive to the 30 acres of gardens, woodland, riparian areas, wetlands, cover crops and wildlife sanctuaries on their Sonoma Mountain estate as they are to the 42 acres planted to winegrapes.
Photograph by M.J. Wickham

Right: The caves at Benziger are naturally climate controlled and the perfect setting for leisurely tasting the flagship wines.
Photograph by M.J. Wickham

Benziger is not just making green wines—the team is making excellent wines. The crew caps more than 20 bottlings a year from some 300 vineyard blocks, all under the wine family of Benziger Family, Benziger Single Vineyard, Signaterra by Benziger, de Coelo, which is the estate pinot noir, and Tribute, which is the estate Bordeaux blend. Each tier of the Benziger portfolio represents the distinctive vineyards where the grapes are grown. From the site-specific Signaterra line of wines to the certified-Biodynamic brands Tribute and de Coelo, the Benzigers are committed to crafting wines with a sense of place.

Coming to the winery, a visitor is immediately immersed in the world of a real working vineyard. Guests can explore Benziger's Sonoma Mountain estate through one of two tours. The first is sort of a Wine 101, where a tram takes visitors through the Biodynamic vineyard, and the methods of production are shown, along with a visit to the wine caves. The second tour is geared toward the wine connoisseur and is a great behind-the-scenes look into the crafting of the Benziger wines.

Top Left: Benziger Family Winery is truly a family affair. Over two-dozen family members live on or around the property, located in Glen Ellen. And the next generation of Benzigers is being groomed to take the helm of the family business.
Photograph courtesy of Benziger Family Winery

Middle Left: Benziger Family Winery's tasting room offers a variety of options—from the Vintner's Menu, featuring a variety of Sonoma County AVA wines, to the Reserve Tasting of small production and rare wines. The tasting room is open daily from 10 a.m. to 5 p.m.
Photograph by M.J. Wickham

Bottom Left: Two types of tours are offered at Benziger Family Winery: the Biodynamic Tram Tour, featuring a close-up look at the Biodynamic vineyards, a visit to the fermentation facility and a walk through the barrel caves, and the Partners Tour, designed specially for wine enthusiasts, providing a behind-the-scenes vineyard tour and exclusive seated wine tasting.
Photograph by M.J. Wickham

Facing Page: Caves located on the Benziger property not only offer the perfect environment for aging wine, but also offer an elegant backdrop for winemaker dinners, events and private parties.
Photograph by M.J. Wickham

Benziger Family Winery has always focused on crafting wines that the family loves—even the sister label, Imagery Estate Winery, explores the possibilities behind fantastically interesting varietals. With the Benziger Family Winery looking out toward the remarkable panorama of wine country, the family tree has certainly established its roots.

BENZIGER
FAMILY WINERY

WINE & FARE

2007 Sangiacomo Vineyard Chardonnay
Pair with sautéed scallops with light cream sauce.

2006 Signaterra Pinot Noir, Bella Luna Vineyard
Pair with leg of lamb with red wine au jus.

2006 Tribute
(certified Biodynamic estate-Bordeaux blend)
Pair with filet mignon and roasted fingerling potatoes.

Tastings
Open to the public daily, year-round

C. Donatiello Winery

Healdsburg

There is no really great translation of the French word *terroir*. "Sense of place" comes closest, and to get a good taste of the earth—goût de terroir—wine has the ability to transcend geography by taking little representative bits of the earth wherever they need to go, agents in the palliative winemaking industry. And no wine transports it origins to the glass better than pinot noir. For this reason, Sonoma County is a great spot to experience terroir. The geology is diverse, so the county has a lot to offer. The Russian River came out of the last ice age, as did the nutrient rich soils. Because of that, some of the most remarkable fruit can be grown here. C. Donatiello Winery sits along what has become known as America's "Gold Coast" of chardonnay and pinot noir grape growing. Soils, sun and fog come together to make up the territory's terroir. The result is distinctive wine, unique to this particular area. The Russian River is a fine illustration of why California is now the vanguard of modern winemaking.

Chris Donatiello came from the East Coast to Sonoma County with the goal of creating pinot noirs and chardonnays that were highly individualistic representations of the vivid Russian River Valley fruit. Chris chose the perfect spot. While Sonoma County is known for great pinot, pinot is known to be a very fickle grape. He will tell you that pinot remembers everything you do and holds a grudge. Along with winemaker Webster Marquez, the winery uses a gentle, hands-on approach in crafting C. Donatiello wines. After acquiring the winery, the team updated the facility from the bottom up; new floor, new lights and everything in between. A cold box is used to chill grapes overnight before the winemaking begins. Cold grapes have less pressure on their skins, thus protecting them from breaking and releasing their precious juice. The winemaking team also instituted gravity-flow methods, hand-sorting, and high-tech de-stemming. Grapes are pressed in a pneumatic basket press, and the wine is aged exclusively in French oak.

Top Left: Owner Chris Donatiello founded the winery right in the Russian River Valley.

Bottom Left: Pinot noir from the Floodgate Vineyard bottling sits in the C. Donatiello tasting room.

Facing Page: Organic farming is found in the garden at C. Donatiello and in Maddie's Vineyard just beyond.
Photographs by Todd Tankersley

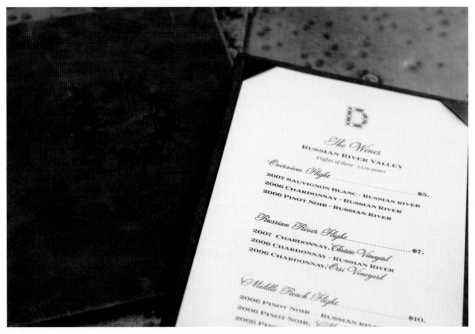

In a way, C. Donatiello Winery is updating to get more traditional. By moving toward high-tech mechanisms and digital controls, the winery becomes gentler in its process.

Balance is of utmost importance. Not too much wood, acid, fruit or tannin. A good wine is well rounded and feels right as it glides across your palate. By keeping a tight rein on everything, the winemaker reveals his passion to create distinctive wines. Focusing on micro-climates in single vineyards, the winery can exemplify the terroir of certain spots. Maddie's Vineyard, an estate vineyard located right on the winery's property, is a certified-organic vineyard and is the crown jewel of the C. Donatiello portfolio. It is the perfect spot for a wine to begin its pilgrimage to the state-of-the-art fermentation room, cellaring and finally bottling. This is true vine-to-wine safeguarding of worth, and the wine, as such, is controlled and captivating, incomparable in its expressions.

Top Left: Members of C. Donatiello's Cellar Guild have access to the private tasting room.
Photograph by Todd Tankersley

Middle Left: Wine is tasted in flights to allow guests to explore the effect each vineyard site has on the wine.
Photograph by Todd Tankersley

Bottom Left: The deck at dusk is the perfect way to end a day of wine tasting.
Photograph by Todd Tankersley

Facing Page: Spring in the organic aroma garden is enhanced in the picnic area.
Photograph by Todd Tankersley

Previous Pages: In the aroma garden guests are encouraged to taste and smell the flora with wine in hand.
Photograph by Todd Tankersley

Of course, the experience of a great wine is always enhanced with a visit to the estate. C. Donatiello Winery has developed aroma gardens to augment the views and the wine itself. Designed to reflect the aromas of pinot noir and chardonnay, the garden can assist in developing your sense of smell to distinguish various aromas in the wine's bouquet. Visitors often walk the garden, glass of wine in hand, picking, smelling and tasting their way through. The tranquility is also a draw. Moving through the gardens or taking a tour through the vineyards, visitors find for themselves the balance that C. Donatiello Winery strives to elicit in each bottle of pinot noir or chardonnay. Passion and knowledge commingle with terroir, and the result is very much a good taste of the earth.

WINE & FARE

Maddie's Vineyard Pinot Noir
(100% pinot noir)
Pair with grilled duck with raspberry foam.

Orsi Vineyard Chardonnay
(100% chardonnay)
Pair with creamy oyster soup with spinach and crème fraiche.

Tastings
Open to the public daily, year-round

Charles Creek Vineyards

Sonoma

Charles Creek Vineyards is one of those rare institutions born of a strong American heritage. Bill Brinton is a direct descendant of John Deere, and there are few iconic names that represent such a long tradition of innovation. After years of successful grape growing in the region, the Brintons—Bill along with his wife, Gerry—founded their own winery in 2002. They have clearly inherited Deere's relentless pursuit for perfection in their winemaking, and the couple works to instill that long history of value and integrity into Charles Creek Vineyards. These are cornerstone ideals that, along with winemaker Kerry Damskey, the Brintons use to produce their award-winning wines.

Charles Creek Vineyards—named after both a son and a grandfather—creates wines with a view to food pairing. It is, after all, a love of the wine-country lifestyle that brought the Brintons into the business. Wine, accordingly, should be an extension of the meal, and so Charles Creek wines are very fruit forward and food friendly. Part of their shared passion in the lifestyle is meeting people. This is where wine differs from any other agricultural product. This idea of bringing people together was the impetus for the Charles Creek Vineyard Tasting Room and Gallery, located on the plaza in Sonoma. But, of course, the wines do most of the talking. Listed on *Wine Enthusiast*'s Top 100 Wines list, the winery has consistently impressed wine lovers—75 gold medals, some 100 silvers and 14 best-in-class awards bear testimony. Charles Creek Vineyards is Midwestern values manifest in Sonoma's always-exciting wine country.

Top Left: Springtime is always a favorite, especially at the Sangiacomo vineyards in the Sonoma Carneros.
Photograph by Bill Brinton

Middle Left: For Bill and Gerry Brinton, proprietors, heritage is very important.
Photograph courtesy of Charles Creek Vineyards

Bottom Left: Bill and Kerry, the winemaker, get to work in the lab.
Photograph courtesy of Charles Creek Vineyards

Facing Page: A great "secret" is the hillside cabernet sauvignon vineyard.
Photograph by Bill Brinton

Cline Cellars

Sonoma

Fred Cline started Cline Cellars in 1982 after graduating from the agriculture and sciences program at UC Davis. Fred was brought up in Los Angeles where his father was a prominent trial lawyer. But he got his early education in agriculture and developed his passion for winemaking during the summers of his teenage years while working with his grandfather, Valeriano Jacuzzi, one of the seven Jacuzzi brothers on his grandfather's farm in eastern Contra Costa County on the Antioch/Oakley border. Zio Valerio to some, Pa or Nonno to others, and his wife Giuseppina—Zia Pina or Ma—had bought the farm as bare land in the 1920s. They developed it into a working farm with almonds and grapes, among other crops. Valeriano patiently taught farming to many members of the Jacuzzi family as his father, Giovanni, had taught the Jacuzzi brothers in Friuli, Italy. And of course, being an Italian immigrant, he made wine for the family dinners in the basement or cellar of the farmhouse as had been done in the old country.

Cline Cellars focuses on Rhône varietals and zinfandels stemming from some of the oldest, rarest grapevines in California—some more than 100 years old. Mourvèdre, viognier, marsanne, roussanne, carignane: Scattered among disparate viticultural areas like Carneros and Contra Costa County, these unusual varietals are the keys to Cline's production and are the driving forces behind The Rhône Rangers, an organization of which Fred is a co-founder. The Rhône-style wines and the renowned zinfandels are Fred's break from the usual California cabernets. These wines, crafted by Cline's eminent winemaker, Charlie Tsegeletos, are visionary products that truly speak to the sense of place.

Top Left: Cline Cellars promises a great wine-country experience.
Photograph by M.J. Wickham

Bottom Left: One of six spring-fed ponds features a remarkable fountain.
Photograph by M.J. Wickham

Facing Page: The Cline grounds offer great picnic spots.
Photograph by M.J. Wickham

One of the methods Cline Cellars uses to ensure the quality of its wines is its sustainable farming program. Avoiding synthetic pesticides and fertilizers, the viticultural experts overseeing the Cline vineyards develop organic practices that allow the true nature of the soil to play out in the wine while preserving the quality of the fruit. Through the careful use of cover crops and the import of raw, volcanic minerals and organic composts, along with very specific methods of weed and pest control through sheep grazing and sprays of organic sulfur dust, the winery takes care to ensure the health of its vines down to the roots. By being good stewards of the land, Cline Cellars creates healthy vineyards that, of course, are essential to balanced flavorful wines.

The winery and tasting room are literally "on a mission." The temporary home of the last of the California missions, Mission Sonoma, was on the present site of Cline Cellars. Mission Sonoma was built on this site in 1823, the last of a long line of Spanish missions along the coast. Later the mission was relocated to its permanent home in downtown Sonoma. The mission site is honored with a museum housing the models of all of the California missions established by Father Junípero Serra, which were

Top Left: An adobe mission gives a sense of early America.
Photograph by M.J. Wickham

Middle Left: The Wine Club House and tasting area is a perfect spot for sampling Cline wines.
Photograph by M.J. Wickham

Bottom Left: The California Missions Museum brings education of the local area.
Photograph by M.J. Wickham

Facing Page: Cline Cellars offers complimentary tastings at the winery.
Photograph by M.J. Wickham

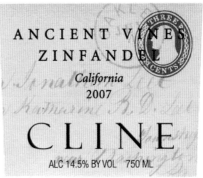

created for and originally shown at the California Pavilion of the 1939 World's Fair on Treasure Island in San Francisco Bay. This is the only collection of scale mission models existing on one site in California and is one of the significant features of Cline Cellars. A nonprofit foundation has been established to house and care for the models. This great educational opportunity is open daily to the public and to the many fourth-grade school children who are required to study California history.

WINE & FARE

Viognier

Pair with Dijon-dill crab cakes or mussels and clams with a shallot-cream sauce.

Marsanne Roussanne

Pair with mild cheeses, citrus-dressed salads, Dover sole or veal with lemon-butter sauces.

Cashmere
(grenache, syrah, mourvèdre)

Pair with roasted poultry, veal or pork.

Mourvèdre

Pair with roasted gamey red meats such as lamb, duck or venison.

Tastings
Open to the public daily, year-round

Davis Bynum Winery

Healdsburg

The first single-vineyard pinot noir came from out of the Russian River Valley in 1973. Produced by Davis Bynum, with grapes from Joe Rochioli's prized vineyard, this pinot began a legacy of excellent wines—chardonnays and a great selection of pinots—that lives on. With continued focus on superb fruit from the Russian River Valley, Davis Bynum produces hand-crafted creations, which themselves sprang from a handshake years ago.

Davis Bynum first flirted with winemaking at home in Berkeley when he was a young reporter working at the *San Francisco Chronicle*. In 1951 he purchased a small amount of petite sirah from Robert Mondavi. Twenty years later, Davis purchased a 26-acre vineyard in Napa Valley with the intention to build a winery. But, because of construction restrictions, he ventured into Sonoma County in 1973, where he found an 84-acre piece of land that quickly became Davis Bynum Winery.

Davis established a quality reputation for the winery, in large part due to solid relationships with the local community of growers. Grapes from great vineyards, often based on handshake agreements, along with "intuitive winemaking," as he refers to it, led the winery to become synonymous with distinctive Russian River Valley pinot noirs and chardonnays. Eventually, acclaim for Bynum wines, along with other area producers, won Russian River Valley recognition as one of the world's very best for these varieties.

Top Left: Winemaker Gary Patzwald heads the Davis Bynum program.
Photograph by Alan Campbell

Bottom Left: Davis Bynum specializes in chardonnay and pinot noir.
Photograph by Alan Campbell

Facing Page: Bynum Vineyard is where it all starts.
Photograph by Alan Campbell

The guiding motivation behind the wines of Davis Bynum Winery is to let the land speak, specifically the terroir of Russian River Valley. The cool maritime conditions of the region are ideally suited for early ripening chardonnay and pinot noir, and finding excellent vineyards within this world-class region continues to drive the style of Bynum wines. The winery determined long ago that its wines should be shaped by the land from which they come.

Nature takes the lead role and the winery's viticultural and winemaking practices fall in line. In both areas, sustainable practices are utilized, which means the grape-growing needs of today are met without threatening the ability of future generations to meet their needs. The three guiding principles are environmental health, economic feasibility and social equity.

Davis Bynum pinot noir is driven by vineyard sites. True to long-established form, it remains a very food-friendly wine, with bright fruit aromas and flavors, a silky texture and a very long finish. The wine is made from a series of exceptional vineyards to create a classic wine that captures all the regional traits. When the winery makes a single-vineyard pinot, it is about capturing the individual terroir of site.

Above: The rolling terrain of Bynum Vineyard enhances fruit flavors.
Photograph by Alan Campbell

Facing Page: From up high, Bynum Vineyard looks out to the mountains.
Photograph by Alan Campbell

The winery's chardonnay comes from the eastern parts of Russian River Valley, nearing Highway 101, where it is just slightly warmer than the very cool western reaches. While maintaining ample crispness, the additional warmth pushes the flavor profile toward tropical and the mouth-feel to a round texture that is lush, but with a clean lingering finish.

In August 2007, ready to retire from the day-to-day activities of running a winery, Davis sold the winery to Tom Klein and the Klein family, a fourth-generation California farming family. The focus on Russian River Valley remains the same, and the goal to produce excellent chardonnay and pinot noir is unchanged.

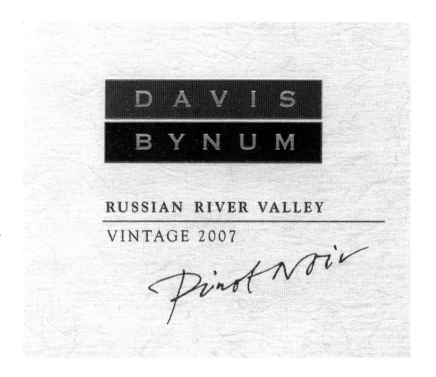

WINE & FARE

Davis Bynum Chardonnay, Russian River Valley
(100% chardonnay)

*Pair with roasted chicken breast with raisins
and pearl couscous.*

Davis Bynum Pinot Noir, Russian River Valley
(100% pinot noir)

*Pair with spinach and bleu cheese salad with sliced apples
and spicy caramelized pecans.*

Tastings
Not open to the public

Deerfield Ranch Winery

Kenwood

"Taste the passion" is the tagline for Deerfield Ranch Winery, founded by PJ and Robert Rex. They have poured their heart and soul into producing clean, high-quality wines from handpicked and hand-sorted grapes grown in sustainable, organic and Biodynamic vineyards. Deerfield Ranch Winery, producing 12,000 cases annually, garnered a seal of approval from California Certified Organic Farmers as one of the few organic-certified producers in Sonoma County.

In the early '70s, PJ left Iowa to continue her education in California. She met Robert, also from Iowa, at UC Berkeley and gave him a winemaking kit for keeping her Alfa Romeo running. Robert, a chemist with the gift of an exceptional palate, was a natural at winemaking. His first vintage, a '72 zinfandel, won best of show at the California State Fair, and he has been taking home the gold ever since.

In 1982 the couple bought Deerfield Ranch in Kenwood, in the heart of Sonoma Valley, and converted a small horse barn into Deerfield Ranch Winery to pursue their passion to make world-class wines. Deerfield Ranch sits atop a ridge overlooking Sonoma Mountain—the inspiration for their logo—and the Alfa can be found parked under the porte-cochere.

"Our winemaking style has its roots in the great French wines of Bordeaux and Burgundy," says Robert. He believes that blending and extended barrel aging create the best wine; grapes from complementary soil types and microclimates are often married to maximize varietal characteristics and complexity. Deerfield's flagship wine is a meritage blend called DRX.

Top Left: Giraffe sculptures stand watch on the island in the wetlands.
Photograph by Patrice Ward

Bottom Left: Tastings are held in the Grand Room in the cave.
Photograph by M.J. Wickham

Facing Page: Deerfield's flagship DRX goes great with food.
Photograph by M.J. Wickham

To honor his Italian heritage, Robert makes a sangiovese and a Tuscan-style wine called Super T-Rex. While the winery produces predominately red wines, it also makes a sauvignon blanc, a chardonnay and a late-harvest botrytis dessert wine called Gold. Renowned for their brilliant color, rich, complex flavors and long finish, Deerfield wines tend to be fruit forward and low in acid, with gentle tannins. They are approachable when young, yet age well. It is Robert's attention to every element of winemaking that makes Deerfield wines stand apart.

In 2000 the Rexes purchased 47 acres next to Deerfield Ranch to expand their production. They built a new winery, planted Biodynamic vineyards, carved a 23,000-square-foot cave into the hillside and built a bioreactor to recycle 98-percent of the winery wastewater. They've spent eight years restoring the 14-acre wetland located on the property. The USDA's Natural Resource Conservation Services teamed up with Deerfield to develop a program to protect the endangered Kenwood Marsh Checkerbloom plant that grows in the wetland. In 2008 the U.S. Fish & Wildlife Service awarded Deerfield Ranch Winery a Certificate of Appreciation for its outstanding contributions to the nation's fish and wildlife resources.

Top Left: Stainless-steel tanks meet French oak barrels in the state-of-the-art winery.
Photograph by Robert Rex

Middle Left: The cave perfectly stores the wines while hosting some fantastic dinners.
Photograph by Patrice Ward

Bottom Left: Robert and Bruno Tison host a food-and-wine pairing in the cave.
Photograph by M.J. Wickham

Facing Page: PJ, Robert and Walker sit with Sonoma Mountain in the background—the inspiration for Deerfield's logo.
Photograph by Malcolm Slight

Robert Rex is a true Renaissance man. Not only is he at the forefront of California winemaking, he also designs the Deerfield labels, can fix almost anything and is an accomplished gourmet cook. Robert and Bruno Tison, Executive Chef for the Fairmont Sonoma Mission Inn, can often be found doing a food-and-wine pairing in the cave or jointly teaching a cooking class at Ramekins Culinary School in Sonoma. PJ Rex, however, may be the backbone of the operation. She has vision and the endurance to make it come true. Deerfield is run by a close-knit group of family members and 10 employees who have developed a reputation for making excellent wines, for being good stewards of the environment and for building a state-of-the-art facility that has become a prime destination in Sonoma Valley.

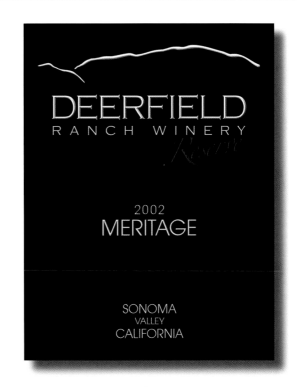

WINE & FARE

Sauvignon Blanc, Peterson Vineyard

Pairs perfectly with oysters on the half shell, shrimp and scallops.

Pinot Noir, Cohn Vineyard

Pairs well with roasted chicken, duck and salmon.

Super T-Rex, Super Tuscan

Pair with pasta with a rich red sauce and grilled meats.

DRX, Meritage Blend

Pairs perfectly with beef or lamb served with a red-wine reduction sauce.

Tastings
Open to the public daily, year-round

deLorimier Vineyards & Winery

Geyserville

Located in the gorgeous Alexander Valley, an appellation renowned for its cabernet sauvignons and chardonnays, deLorimier's vineyards are planted mostly with Bordeaux varieties. When Ken and Diane Wilson bought the winery they were searching for that perfect Alexander Valley property that they could make into their Cabernet House. Often referred to as "California's Bordeaux," the local landscape is itself a genuine mosaic of soil types and microclimates, growing some of the finest grapes in the world, making this a winemaker's dream location for producing world-class wines.

From the estate vineyards, Diane will continue to produce the renowned Crazy Creek Vineyard Cabernet Sauvignon, several chardonnays, cabernets, zinfandel and malbec. The upcoming releases will feature eight single-vineyard-designate cabernet sauvignons, which will honor their vineyards. The impressive gallery tasting room has high ceilings and gorgeous views beyond the tasting bar. The white plastered walls display the work of local artists, all part of the deLorimier gallery experience. Art and wine, the perfect complements, are personified at this premier winery. With two beautiful patios and a private tasting room, the winery is renowned for special events, including weddings. The team at deLorimier brings not only many years of experience, but also a passion that is a key element in the creation of each unique vintage. Whether visitors are playing croquet on the lawn or sitting by the fountain in the cabana courtyard, they will be welcomed with award-winning wines, food-and-wine pairings and a knowledgeable and friendly staff.

Left: Ken and Diane Wilson produce wines that are known for the character of the estate, rather than purely for their varietal content.
Photographs by M.J. Wickham

Facing Page: The hot summer days and fog-cooled nights make the area perfect for creating wines of character and intensity.
Photograph by M.J. Wickham

Above & Left: Furthering the Bordeaux-inspired tradition of the vineyards is the Wilsons' mission.
Photographs by M.J. Wickham

Facing Page: The estate is idyllically set in the center of the northern Alexander Valley.
Photograph by M.J. Wickham

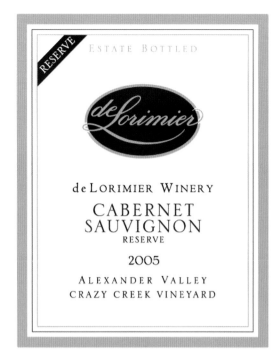

deLorimier's focus is on producing small-lot, vineyard-designate wines that are the purest reflection of the grapes, the land and the process. Total involvement from bud break to bottling ensures that only wines of the highest caliber are represented by the deLorimier brand. The uncompromising dedication to quality and the quest for excellence is what keeps each new vintage vibrant and exciting, and each bottle a pleasure to be savored. The impact of deLorimier is resonating in the premium-wine community, all from the dream of two wine-industry experts. This expertise in crafting the elements of winemaking has created what are arguably some of the finest wines available today.

Wine & Fare

deLorimier Reserve Chardonnay

Pair with a dill-poached salmon on rice with grilled asparagus.

deLorimier Reserve Sauvignon Blanc

Pair with asparagus and artichoke pasta salad with chicken or shrimp.

deLorimier Merlot

Pair with a simmered pot roast with carrots and onions and served with sautéed Brussels sprouts.

Tastings

Open to the public daily, year-round

Dutcher Crossing Winery

Healdsburg

Hailing from Wisconsin, Debra Mathy certainly had a feeling when she looked to the west. Paving a different path than her family's asphalt business, Debra headed to California with the dream of owning a winery. Her father, too, shared her passion, and together they sought to make this dream come true. Debra found a beautiful little spot in Healdsburg at the hills of Dry Creek Valley. Opened in 2005, Dutcher Crossing Winery sets the standard for tasty boutique wines.

Visiting the winery, one understands why Debra journeyed here. The 1900s-era, farmhouse-style winery is quaint, charming and certainly inviting. Tucked away from the more crowded areas of Sonoma County, the winery is the perfect picnic spot in a magnificently pastoral area. Standing in the winery's breezeway, visitors realize very quickly that humanity's ties to nature are intrinsic. The rolling hills of the beautiful Dry Creek Valley are the perfect backdrop to Dutcher Crossing's vineyards. This experience is not restricted to the wine connoisseur and discussions of proper blending; sipping, say, a 2006 Proprietor's Reserve Cabernet and nibbling on some of the winery's seasonal selection of cheeses and breads, there is the distinct feeling of transcendence to some plush paradise, where the only commandment is to relax and enjoy.

Top Left: Debra and Dutchess monitor the Estate Vineyard grapes.
Photograph by M.J. Wickham

Middle Left: A high-spirited Petanque game gets played on the winery court.
Photograph by M.J. Wickham

Bottom Left: Debra Mathy, proprietor, takes in a glass.
Photograph by M.J. Wickham

Facing Page: The original vineyard cabernet sauvignon vines are the foundation of the Proprietor's Reserve Cabernet.
Photograph by M.J. Wickham

Top: The winery solar project was the beginning of the environmental commitment.
Photograph by M.J. Wickham

Bottom: Dutchess takes Debra's spot in the ATV vehicle until Debra returns from the vines.
Photograph by M.J. Wickham

Top: Dutcher Crossing sits approximately 50 yards from the historical crossing of Dry Creek and Dutcher Creek.
Photograph by M.J. Wickham

Bottom: The picnic area is perfect for a serene private tasting.
Photograph by M.J. Wickham

For Debra—who has a business background—the draw to the wine industry is the range of diverse day-to-day activities. One day the focus may be farming or blending, the next marketing and hospitality—cultivating a product that is both public and personal allows for a unique dynamic not found in most careers. When Debra found the site, she felt right at home, but wanted special growth in the vineyards and an elevation of the high-quality wines that were previously produced. The winery had a great foundation, but the proprietor and the winemaker wanted to create more vineyard designates, searching out high-pedigree, unique vineyards to add to the already established valley-floor vineyards. Veteran winemaker Kerry Damskey, a true ambassador for the industry, instills his passion and knowledge into bottles virtually unmatched in American winemaking—kicking a toe into dirt, Kerry can gauge the soil compositions and the grapes that could sprout from the spot.

The key component to enjoying a Dutcher Crossing wine, of course, is drinking it. But while great wines with friends may have been the priority with the winery, Dutcher Crossing also continually strives for higher farming practices, looking for environmentally conscious methods to protect the land on which they work. Besides implementing a Segway Personal Transporter as the roving podium throughout the vineyard, cutting down vast quantities of gas and oil, the winery had SolarCraft design and build a 32kW solar electric system. These roof- and ground-mounted mechanisms generate enough clean energy to power the entire property.

Above Left: The winery breezeway frames the breathtaking vineyard backdrop.
Photograph by M.J. Wickham

Above Right: Dutcher Crossing's outer entrance gardens supply winery guests with strawberries, apples and lavender during visits.
Photograph by M.J. Wickham

Facing Page: Dutcher Crossing wines wait to be poured during a cozy lunch by the winery's outdoor fireplace.
Photograph by M.J. Wickham

The winery's new label, featuring the iconic bicycle, represents a father-daughter journey in wine country and the continued path traveled in crafting premium artisan wines. Dutcher Crossing Winery, after all, is about wine and people. At any point, visitors may run into Debra scooting along on her Segway, or maybe Kerry working with the wine in the barrel room or crush pad. But if you are lucky, Dutchess, the official wine dog of Dutcher Crossing, may have her own tale to tell.

DUTCHER CROSSING

WINE & FARE

2007 Dry Creek Valley Sauvignon Blanc
(94% sauvignon blanc, 3% semillon, 3% viognier)

Pair with tuna tartare, oysters, spicy Asian dishes and cheeses.

2007 Stuhlmuller Vineyard Chardonnay
(100% chardonnay)

Pair with chicken, pasta, cheeses and salads.

2006 Maple Vineyard Zinfandel
(91% zinfandel, 9% petite sirah)

Pair with pork tenderloin, steak and pasta dishes.

2006 Proprietor's Reserve Cabernet
(80% estate cabernet sauvignon, 20% syrah)

Pair this extremely versatile wine with anything from pizza to filet mignon.

Tastings
Open to the public daily, year-round

Ferrari-Carano
Vineyards and Winery

Healdsburg

I n 1987 an unknown winery released two wines—an '86 Fumé Blanc and an '85 Alexander Valley Chardonnay. With these two stellar bottles, the Ferrari-Carano label burst onto the Sonoma County wine scene.

Don and Rhonda Carano were introduced to the beauty of Northern Sonoma County in 1979 while searching for wines to enhance the wine lists at their hotel, the Eldorado Hotel and Casino, established in 1973, in Reno, Nevada. Eventually the couple purchased a 70-acre parcel in Alexander Valley. The vineyards piqued their curiosity about winemaking, and so they began taking classes on enology and viticulture. The wine they made in their barn was bottled under the Carano Cellars label and was given to friends and family, eventually appearing on the wine lists at the Eldorado. Realizing the potential that this area held, the Caranos began to acquire additional vineyard land, subsequently founding Ferrari-Carano Vineyards and Winery in 1981.

The winery incorporates the word "vineyards" as a deliberate emphasis on the important role of grape source and terroir in the final, bottled product. From the small plot of grapes bought in 1979 to today's 20 estate vineyards in five appellations—Dry Creek Valley, Russian River Valley, Alexander Valley, Napa/Carneros and Anderson Valley—totaling 1,600 acres, Ferrari-Carano owns some of the finest wine growing properties in all of California. Ferrari-Carano vineyard practices are customized to match the particular characteristics of each vineyard to help the vines produce the best fruit possible and, in turn, to achieve the best wine possible. Directed by Don Carano and orchestrated under

Top Left: Don and Rhonda Carano, owners of Ferrari-Carano, discovered Sonoma County while searching for wines to serve at their hotel-casino.
Photograph courtesy of Ferrari-Carano Vineyards and Winery

Bottom Left: Ferrari-Carano's family of wines includes the Chardonnay Reserve from Napa/Carneros and Trésor, a Bordeaux-style blend from Alexander Valley.
Photograph courtesy of Ferrari-Carano Vineyards and Winery

Facing Page: The Villa Fiore hospitality center in Dry Creek Valley is open daily and features five acres of lush gardens, spectacular vineyard views, a wine shop and two wine-tasting bars.
Photograph by M.J. Wickham

the supervision of Steve Domenichelli, Director of Vineyard Operations, these practices are extremely labor intensive. Steve and his team implement nutrient regimes, trellis system and canopy management, rootstock and clone combinations and pruning and cane selection for each vineyard site and each block within a vineyard. Because of Sonoma County's diverse geological makeup, even within one vineyard parcel there may be several different types of soil with different degrees of nutrients for vines and water-holding capacity.

Ferrari-Carano has long practiced sustainable farming techniques to help protect the lands it farms—both vineyard and agriculture—and the environment that surrounds them. Don and Rhonda Carano realized early on that to achieve their goal of producing memorable wines of outstanding quality, they needed to start in the vineyards and not focus solely on the

winemaking. Inspired to meet their present goals while preserving the land for future generations, Don and Rhonda implemented techniques such as fish-friendly farming and utilizing a tree sap alternative to asphalt on the mountain ranch roads and have made essential contributions to biodiversity, nutrient recycling and waste management.

Above: Ferrari-Carano's LookOut Mountain Ranch sits high above the valley at the apex of Alexander, Chalk Hill and Knights Valleys.
Photograph by M.J. Wickham

Right: In Ferrari-Carano's underground cellar's Enotec Bar, visitors enjoy tasting limited-release and reserve wines. Private tastings are available by appointment.
Photograph courtesy of Ferrari-Carano Vineyards and Winery

Facing Page Bottom: Don and Rhonda Carano's private cellar is located in the Enoteca Bar and Lounge.
Photograph by M.J. Wickham

But the wine is the kicker. There are two distinct winemaking teams at Ferrari-Carano. Sarah Quider is the winemaker for the white wines, including the pinot grigio, sauvignon blanc and chardonnay. Sarah and her team search for quality in every bottle, employing gentle winemaking techniques, keeping all lots separate and then blending wine for style, quality and the multidimensional complexity that characterizes Ferrari-Carano wine. Aaron Piotter is the winemaker for the red wines, which are produced at Ferrari-Carano's magnificent Mountain Winery Estate, one of the most scenic properties in Sonoma County. The Mountain Winery's uniquely designed, eco-sensitive grape delivery system allows for meticulous hand sorting of grapes for maximum quality control, while incorporating gravity flow delivery to French-oak fermenters. The wine caves, with natural temperature and humidity ranges, create the ideal environment for barrel aging and ensure an end result of wines of incredible richness and complexity. All of Ferrari-Carano 's red wines are made and aged here, including merlot, zinfandel, cabernet sauvignon, Siena, Trésor, PreVail West Face and PreVail Back Forty.

Visiting Ferrari-Carano's winery estate in picturesque Dry Creek Valley is truly a special treat. Visitors may take in panoramic vineyard views while tasting world-renowned, classic wines in the wine shop or head downstairs to the Enoteca Bar in the underground

Top Left: Ferrari-Carano's spectacular LookOut Mountain Ranch in Alexander Valley boasts 360-degree views of Sonoma and Napa counties.
Photograph courtesy of Ferrari-Carano Vineyards and Winery

Middle Left: The underground barrel cellar at Villa Fiore provides the perfect conditions for aging Ferrari-Carano's wines.
Photograph courtesy of Ferrari-Carano Vineyards and Winery

Bottom Left: Private tastings, available by appointment, are hosted in The PreVail Room, located in Ferrari-Carano's Enoteca Bar.
Photograph by M.J. Wickham

Facing Page: Ferrari-Carano's beautiful gardens are open daily to the public, year-round, and feature a dazzling display of flowers, shrubs and trees.
Photograph courtesy of Ferrari-Carano Vineyards and Winery

cellar to sample reserve and limited-release wines. Guests won't want to miss a stroll through the five acres of lush, award-winning gardens, featuring meandering footpaths and streams, waterfalls and a dazzling display of color, no matter the time of year. Tours are by appointment, and private group wine tastings are available. In addition, guests may join Ferrari-Carano's Circle of Friends Wine Club and enjoy Ferrari-Carano wines delivered right to their doors.

From two wines 25 years ago, Ferrari-Carano Vineyards and Winery continues to produce world-class wines without compromise, a fortunate creation for the rest of us.

WINE & FARE

Ferrari-Carano Fumé Blanc, Sonoma County
(100% sauvignon blanc)
Pair with spicy lime ginger grilled shrimp.

Ferrari-Carano Chardonnay, Alexander Valley
(100% chardonnay)
Pair with pasta butterflies with asparagus and snow peas.

Ferrari-Carano Siena, Sonoma County
(68% sangiovese, 32% malbec)
Pair with chicken cacciatore.

**Ferrari-Carano Cabernet Sauvignon,
Alexander Valley**
*(88% cabernet sauvignon, 4% syrah, 4% cabernet franc,
4% petit verdot)*
Pair with grilled marinated London broil.

PreVail Back Forty, Alexander Valley
(100% cabernet sauvignon)
*Pair with grilled rosemary-infused brochette of lamb
with mission figs.*

Tastings
Open to the public daily, year-round

Fisher Vineyards

Mayacamas Mountains

Founded in 1973 by Fred and Juelle Fisher, Fisher Vineyards is a true family-owned and -operated winery. Today all three of Fred and Juelle's children, Whitney, Robert and Cameron, have joined the winery and are leading the way to a second generation of world-class wines produced from their two properties—Napa Valley Estate in Calistoga and Spring Mountain Estate in Sonoma County.

With a mission to produce cabernet and chardonnay wines that express their unique mountain or valley heritage, Fisher Vineyards pays tribute to the land, with wines showing classic balance and style that transcend time.

Fisher Vineyards' flagship wine, the Coach Insignia Cabernet Sauvignon, derives its name from the Fisher Body Company—founded in 1908 by the seven Fisher brothers of Detroit, including Fred's grandfather. The Fisher Body Company's logo, referred to as the Coach Insignia, represented the artistry and luxury of an unhurried age and was the standard of extraordinary craftsmanship in automobiles for much of the 20th century.

Fisher Vineyards seeks to continue the tradition of the Coach Insignia by producing a wine that justly embodies craftsmanship, artistry and luxury.

Top Left: The Fisher family includes Juelle, Cameron, Fred, Rob and Whitney.
Photograph by M.J. Wickham

Bottom Left: A private tasting in the Madrone Grove is paired with a seasonal menu designed around the bounty of fruit, produce and herbs grown on the property.
Photograph by M.J. Wickham

Facing Page: Estate vineyards planted on steep mountain slopes reach elevations of more than 1,400 feet.
Photograph by M.J. Wickham

Above: Old chardonnay vines are netted in late summer to protect them from birds. As fruit ripens each season throughout the Mountain Estate, all vines are netted by hand when the time is right.
Photograph by M.J. Wickham

Right: Fisher Vineyards follows sustainable-farming methods to maintain vibrant, balanced vineyards that produce small quantities of the highest-quality fruit.
Photograph by M.J. Wickham

Facing Page Bottom: The winery, designed by the late William Turnbull, was constructed entirely from redwood and Douglas-fir trees grown and milled on the Mountain Estate.
Photograph by M.J. Wickham

Over the years Fisher wines have been crafted by three stellar winemakers, starting with Chuck Ortman, followed by Paul Hobbs and most recently Mia Klein. Mia mentored the Fishers' daughter Whitney, who became winemaker in 2003. Today Whitney oversees the estate vineyards while directing the wine production; she is joined by consulting enologist Aaron Pott.

The family has worked closely with David Abreu, a prominent viticulturalist, for vineyard replanting. With each new development, the Fishers remain committed to planting vineyards following cutting-edge techniques and farming sustainably with their own vineyard management crew, led by the same family for more than 35 years.

To visit Fisher Vineyards is to be invited into the Fishers' home for a truly unique experience. The winery is a product of the estate, having been built from timber that was grown, cut and milled onsite, then crafted into an award-wining facility by the Fishers' good friend and architect, the late William Turnbull.

Above Left: Custom-milled Douglas-fir beams buttress high ceilings, creating lofty space above fermentation tanks.
Photograph by M.J. Wickham

Above Right: All wines are aged in French oak barrels, cellared in deep underground caves and watched over carefully by Whitney and the wine team.
Photograph by M.J. Wickham

Facing Page: Visiting Fisher Vineyards is an intimate affair—meeting family members and enjoying memorable tastings of limited-production and even library wines.
Photograph by M.J. Wickham

Any visit, tasting or meal at the winery, whether under the Madrone Grove or perched mid-mountain on The Terrace, awakens the senses to the earthly greatness of estate-grown food and wine—it is the kind of experience that can only be discovered in such seclusion.

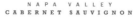

2005

COACH INSIGNIA

NAPA VALLEY
CABERNET SAUVIGNON

WINE & FARE

Whitney's Vineyard, Chardonnay

Pair with a purée of sweet carrots with curried crème fraîche.

Cameron, Bordeaux Blend

Pair with braised porkbelly on spiced butternut squash.

Coach Insignia, Cabernet Sauvignon

Pair with grilled medallions of lamb with mint couscous and spring onions.

Wedding Vineyard, Cabernet Sauvignon

Pair with braised wagyu short ribs with celery-root purée, forest mushrooms and spinach.

Tastings
Open by appointment only

Foppiano Vineyards

Healdsburg

W.C. Fields said, "Once, during Prohibition, I had to live for days on nothing but food and water." Not everybody is a drinker, but if Prohibition taught us anything, it is that we like having the option. In 1926 federal agents popped into Foppiano Vineyards and enhanced the earthy flavors of the family's 1918 vintage by cutting the tank valves and dumping some 100,000 gallons of wine into the winery's creek. People came from miles around with cups and jugs to taste a sample of the Foppiano label. Deny us, and we will sprawl creekside; if it happens to be a product of Foppiano Vineyards, so much the better.

Giovanni Foppiano came to America in the mid-1850s, following the rush to gold. Looking for something more fruitful, Giovanni moved into winemaking. He bought the Riverside Farm winery in Sonoma County, establishing it as Foppiano Vineyards in 1896. Soon, Giovanni's son Louis A. joined the action, beginning a family line for Foppiano Vineyards, managed now by Louis M. Foppiano—the fourth-generation and third Louis Foppiano at the helm of one of the country's few six-generation family operations. Foppiano Vineyards survived Prohibition by adding prunes, apples and pears to its crop growing, and by shipping grapes for homemade wines—a little loophole in the law that allowed the people to make some of their own. A century later, Foppiano Vineyards still maintains that initial determination and dedication that the winery was founded on—a family epic that spans the 20th century and beyond.

Top Left: Foppiano Vineyards spans generations. Susan Valera and Louis M. stand, while Louis J., Giana and Paul sit in the winery picnic area.
Photograph by M.J. Wickham

Bottom Left: The 17-year-old petite sirah vine is ready to harvest.
Photograph by M.J. Wickham

Facing Page: From the tasting room, views look out over the petite sirah toward the Russian River.
Photograph by M.J. Wickham

Top: The winery entrance is located on Old Redwood Highway.
Photograph by M.J. Wickham

Bottom: The winery's cellar door is a great throwback to traditional
winery architecture.
Photograph by M.J. Wickham

Top: An old Northwestern Pacific Railroad caboose finds a new use as the winery's office space.
Photograph by M.J. Wickham

Bottom: The winery's old horse barn was built in the late 1800s.
Photograph by M.J. Wickham

History is important, but change is vital. In the 1960s the demand for premium wines increased, and so Foppiano Vineyards embraced the shift by moving from its famous jug wines into specific varietals, such as cabernet sauvignon, pinot noir and the family favorite, petite sirah. The move to new technology, including stainless-steel fermenting tanks, and the implementation of oak barrels, clearly illustrates the winery's commitment to quality wine. However, modern technology is not an end in itself. Gentleness always produces the best wines.

The Foppiano Ranch sits on 160 acres of Russian River benchland, of which 132 are vineyards. Maintaining the vineyards is Raul Guerrero, who joined in 1975 after literally running out of gas in front of the winery, and Paul Foppiano, fifth generation, who came aboard in 1999. This viticultural team pushes to produce grapes that can be counted on to impress continually. But with other Foppianos on hand, including

Louis J., a pioneer in the industry and the current president, and Susan Foppiano Valera, a passionate outdoorswoman and hospitality manager, the winery includes everybody with a vested interest in cultivating marvelous grapes and turning them into beautiful wines.

Above Left: The bar area in the tasting room offers a rustic appeal.
Photograph by M.J. Wickham

Above Right: Below photos of Louis A. and his wife Matilda hang the many awards and medals that the winery has received.
Photograph by M.J. Wickham

Facing Page: The Margot Patterson Doss self-guided walk through the vineyards is a great place to experience wine country.
Photograph by M.J. Wickham

With two labels, Foppiano Vineyards and Lot 96, the winery is able to maximize the potential that stems from the grapes, exclusively dedicating the former label to reds. Dropping in at the winery's tasting room, one can see why Foppiano Vineyards is Sonoma County's oldest, continually operated, family-owned vineyard—for a wine that tastes this good must be a survivor.

WINE & FARE

2007 Pinot Grigio, Napa Valley
(100% pinot grigio)

Pair with grilled chicken salad with plum vinaigrette.

2006 Pinot Noir, Russian River Estate
(100% pinot noir)

*Pair with grilled lamb chops basted
in sesame garlic honey glaze.*

2005 Petite Sirah, Russian River Valley Estate
(100% petite sirah)

Pair with chocolate biscotti.

Tastings
Open to the public daily, year-round

Freeman Vineyard & Winery

Sebastopol

Once known as the Gravenstein Apple Capital of the World, Sebastopol in Sonoma County is now home to an incredible region of pinot noir grapes and wine production due to its ideal climate conditions.

It is here that Freeman Vineyard & Winery has its roots. The characteristics of the area coupled with the charm and quality of the property make its location prime for the production of the owners' favorite wines: pinot noir and chardonnay. Practicing the best of Burgundy's winemaking techniques in the climate and geology of California's coastal mountains, the Freemans use this terroir to craft what critics have called some of the finest wines in the world.

Ken and Akiko Freeman both grew up in food and wine households, but on opposite sides of the globe. Ken, a native New Yorker and skilled business and investment banker, developed a passion for wine at the age of 10 after visiting the cork trees of Portugal with his family. Conversely, Akiko spent the first part of her life in Tokyo. Akiko's grandfather, one of Japan's leading academics, instilled in her a love of life's finer things—literature, art, food and, of course, wine. She came to America in 1985 and met Ken quickly thereafter. The couple unified their passions for wine and began their search for a winery that would make stylistically different wines in the Burgundy and Bordeaux traditions.

Top Left: Ken and Akiko Freeman stand at the entrance to the wine cave.
Photograph by M.J. Wickham

Bottom Left: Akiko's Cuvee and Ryo-fu Chardonnay are some of Freeman's finest.
Photograph by M.J. Wickham

Facing Page: The rolling hills of Freeman Ranch Vineyard are in Occidental, California.
Photograph by M.J. Wickham

As a principle, Ken and Akiko Freeman make what they like to drink. The wines that come from Freeman Vineyard & Winery are small-lot wines, handpicked from separated blocks. Winemaker Ed Kurtzman came to Freeman from highly esteemed wineries to work with the passionate duo. Contracted with some of the leading growers in the region, the winery gets most of its fruit from the mountains, for the flavors there are much bigger.

Their specific practices, such as picking the fruit at night to keep the grapes cool, mean that Mother Nature is allowed to express her best qualities in Freeman's wines. The wine itself has been described as having a feminine touch, mostly due to Akiko's influence on the process.

The French have always said that wine is grown in the vineyards. The elegance and balance of Freeman's wines verifies that the winery's selection process is phenomenal. High elevations combined with some of California's remarkable redwoods create an ecosystem bar none in the American wine industry, and truly beyond; one of the top exporters of wine to Japan, Freeman Vineyard & Winery is dedicated to creating food-friendly wine full of depth and character.

Top Left: The entrance of the Freeman wine cave is a great place to start a tour.
Photograph by M.J. Wickham

Bottom Left: Inside the wine cave is where the magic happens.
Photograph by M.J. Wickham

Facing Page: The redwood grove at Freeman Winery offers a great tranquil spot.
Photograph by M.J. Wickham

Freeman Vineyard & Winery encapsulates Sonoma County with outstanding bottles, proving that a dream can be made manifest when it is propelled by enthusiasm and passion.

FREEMAN
VINEYARD & WINERY

WINE & FARE

Akiko's Cuvee, Sonoma Coast, Pinot Noir
(100% pinot noir)

*Pair with mushrooms, lamb chops, poultry
and flavorful seafood.*

Ryo-fu, "Cool Breeze" Russian River, Chardonnay
(100% chardonnay)

*Pair with lobster, scallops, other mild-flavored
seafood and poultry.*

Tastings
Open by appointment only

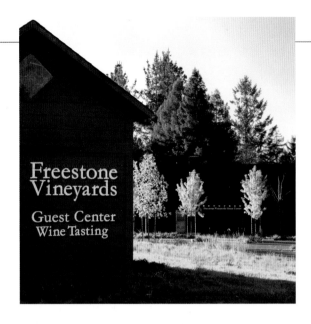

Freestone Vineyards

After establishing a successful Napa winery, the Phelps family headed west in search of chardonnay, a grape that required a cooler environment to thrive. But this effort evolved to something much greater as the crew settled in with Freestone Vineyards: A pinot noir wave washed through the wine-drinking world, and the Freestone crew had an excellent opportunity to produce pinot noir grapes from one of the world's top spots for that varietal. By growing what would work best in its vineyards, Freestone was able to produce wine that reflects the unique corner of Sonoma Coast. Though a reflection of the Burgundy wine style, Freestone Vineyards exemplifies that which is most fascinating in California wine country.

Located in the town of Freestone, the winery intended on joining a vibrant, fun community that would elevate the wine experience. Theresa Heredia, Freestone's winemaker, is tasked with capturing in each bottle the elements of the vineyards, the experience of terroir. Produced in the Burgundian style, the pinot noir and chardonnay grapes are products of art and science. Looking for overall balance and structure in the wine, the Freestone crew is comfortable experimenting and trying new things—using something like wooden fermenting tanks may cause a decrease in temperature control, but the structure that results is worth the extra effort.

Top Left: The guest center, in the background, is a neighbor to the little barn that was on the site.
Photograph by M.J. Wickham

Middle Left: The guest center features casual seating and a cozy stove.
Photograph by M.J. Wickham

Bottom Left: A copper countertop welcomes guests for tastings.
Photograph by M.J. Wickham

Facing Page: The northwest panorama is an idyllic viewpoint at Freestone Vineyards.
Photograph by M.J. Wickham

Biodynamic farming plays a great role in Freestone's operations. Combining natural farming practices with some more eclectic, natural remedies ensures that the land itself remains a self-sustaining property, producing wines that are as natural as possible by keeping the land close to pre-industrial days. With three distinct vineyards—Pastorale, Quarter Moon and Ferguson—Freestone Vineyards lets the Earth speak through the creation of its products.

While Freestone maintains a brand-new, state-of-the-art winery, its guest center was substantially renovated from an existing building—Freestone, therefore, remains warm and welcoming, summer and winter.

Top Left: Looking down at the entrance to the winery, one can see the crush pad and sorting area.
Photograph by M.J. Wickham

Middle Left: To the east, a demonstration of the winery's gravity flow system can be seen.
Photograph by M.J. Wickham

Bottom Left: West and south, Freestone Vineyards is a remarkable landscape.
Photograph by M.J. Wickham

Facing Page: Table seating in the guest center makes for a perfect evening.
Photograph by M.J. Wickham

Though 88 percent of the winery's vineyards produce pinot noir grapes, each wine that the winery bottles is a product of its spot—the perfect commingling of cool climate, ancient soils and hillside elevations. Terroir is the stacking of these elements, and Freestone uses such geological phenomena to the benefit of wine drinkers. The Fogdog label, for instance, is named after the meteorological clearing in a fog bank, which offers an ideal respite from the haze.

With the new guest center in place, Freestone Vineyards utilizes Burgundian principles to elevate the plane of great California wine.

Freestone

2007
PINOT NOIR
SONOMA COAST

WINE & FARE

Freestone Chardonnay
Pair with frittata with mushrooms, sweet onion and Gruyère cheese.

Ovation Chardonnay
Pair with rosemary and lemon shrimp.

Fogdog Chardonnay
Pair with velvety mushroom soup.

Freestone Pinot Noir
Pair with mushroom risotto.

Tastings
Open to the public, Friday, Saturday and Sunday, year-round

Gary Farrell Vineyards & Winery

Healdsburg

Call them visionaries. Groundbreakers. A little compulsive. Maybe a bit crazy. But way back in the late 1970s, a handful of winemakers had the idea of growing pinot noir in the Russian River Valley. Today those names are legendary for having established one of the world's most celebrated regions. In 1982 one of those original pioneers, Gary Farrell, produced his first wines—50 cases of pinot noir from the Rochioli and Allen vineyards. The rest, as they say, is history.

Today winemaker Susan Reed, who produced several vintages side-by-side with Gary, has seamlessly extended and built upon a storied tradition of excellence. To Susan, it's all about protecting the integrity of the fruit. "My goal is to continue the tradition of creating world-class wines," she says, "wines that evoke the uniqueness of the vineyard from which they were produced."

The Russian River's inexorable fog is the key to the region's prominence in pinot noir and chardonnay. The Pacific Ocean and Russian River influences help stabilize temperature throughout the entire region, allowing for a slow ripening process that results in fruit with a bright and vibrant natural acidity, remarkable balance and delightful flavor intensity.

Gary Farrell Winery benefits immeasurably from its long-term relationships with many of the Russian River Valley's most celebrated vineyards, including Rochioli, Allen, Hallberg and Westside Farms, to name a few. These are among the very best of the best in an AVA rich in stunning vineyard sites. And taken collectively, they create the foundation for wines that speak to the unlimited potential of the Russian River Valley.

Top Left: The sun burns off the fog mid-morning at Rochioli Vineyard.
Photograph by Chris Poulsen

Middle Left & Facing Page: The tasting room entrance perched atop a hillside has breathtaking views overlooking Sonoma County's Russian River Valley. Each offering in the family of wines is bright and crisp, with subtle layers of flavor that unfold on the palate.
Photographs by Chris Poulsen

Bottom Left: The barrel room is a reflection of an artisan's uncompromising attention to detail.
Photograph by Chris Poulsen

America is adept at pushing the boundaries of the possible through science and technology. This idea can be seen in vast projects like the space race, but also in more earthbound endeavors, such as winemaking. In 1948 Harry Truman sent Ambassador James D. Zellerbach to Italy to implement the famed Marshall Plan. Zellerbach returned from this vast restructuring venture with some new ideas for restructuring the development of wine. Those great, Grand Cru Burgundy wines—known for astonishing quality and immense endurance—should have serious competition in California, where, at the time, only a few hundred acres of chardonnay vineyards were maintained. Though the Ambassador held to the traditions of those Burgundies, he knew that tradition was not enough in the New World, that science and technology would revolutionize winemaking in America.

In 1953 Zellerbach invested part of his family's paper-manufacturing fortune in the planting of four acres of pinot noir—now the oldest pinot noir vineyard in America—and two acres of chardonnay. He hired on the talented Brad Webb as winemaker, and soon they built a winery that operated by a gravity-feed process modeled after the 12th-century press building at Clos de Vougeot in Burgundy. The two sought the latest technology, installing the first jacketed, stainless-steel fermenting tanks in the industry—marking the first time that wine temperature could be completely controlled by the makers. To recall the flavor of Burgundy, Zellerbach introduced aging of his wines in small, French oak barrels, instead of the large redwood casks that were the California norm. This was not the only measurable improvement. Brad, having an extensive scientific education, understood that oxidation causes wines to mature and speeds deterioration. Blanketing

Top Left: Hanzell Vineyards' de Brye Vineyard holds pinot noir grapes right before harvest.
Photograph by M.J. Wickham

Bottom Left: Hanzell wines are designed to hold their own against classic Burgundies.
Photograph by M.J. Wickham

Facing Page: Hanzell Vineyards Heritage Winery was built in 1957 and operated by a gravity-feed process.
Photograph by M.J. Wickham

young wines in inert gas, such as nitrogen, would ensure longevity, so he developed specialized fittings that introduced contact with nitrogen, a process that is now widespread in the industry. As well, he figured out a way to control the then-mysterious occurrence of malolactic fermentation. Inducing and controlling this secondary fermentation prior to bottling was pioneered at Hanzell and, because of the Ambassador's generous principles, shared with all winemakers. These processes mark the groundbreaking moments of what the Ambassador dubbed Hanzell Vineyards—a contraction of his wife's name, Hana Zellerbach.

In the years hence, stewardship of Hanzell Vineyards passed from the Zellerbachs to Douglas and Mary Day in the '60s, then to Barbara de Brye in the '70s. Now her son, Alexander de Brye, has a very clear goal for it. The hallmark of a great wine is ageability, and Hanzell strives to produce wines that benefit from additional time in the bottle. A well-aged Hanzell wine can sit proudly on the same table as a 20-year-old Burgundy. This happens for two reasons. An early pioneer in wine research, Hanzell Vineyards continues to experiment with both tannin development and an in-depth study of balance in young wine.

Left: Hanzell Vineyards' stainless-steel fermentation tanks wait in their new, technically advanced production area.
Photograph by M.J. Wickham

Facing Page Left: Michael McNeill, winemaker; Ben Sessions, estate educator; Jean Arnold Sessions, president; and Alexander de Brye, owner.
Photographs by M.J. Wickham

Facing Page Right: A lovely place to enjoy a glass of Hanzell Vineyards chardonnay with friends is overlooking the de Brye Vineyard.
Photograph by M.J. Wickham

The estate itself is considered a *monopole*—a literal monopoly by a single vineyard over a distinct area. The winery's property is in its own defined geographical area. A unique combination of geology and climate means that only Hanzell produces wine from this specific site—the essence of monopole. The chardonnay and pinot noir vines found here have been producing for more than 50 years, and this fundamental understanding of the distinctive estate vineyards creates a Hanzell chardonnay that can typically age 20 years.

Now the winery lovingly tends 46 acres of vineyards on 200 acres of private property, under the masterful hands of winemaker emeritus Bob Sessions—who joined Hanzell in 1973—and current winemaker Michael McNeill. President Jean Arnold Sessions has orchestrated the production of 6,000 cases annually, three-quarters dedicated to chardonnay and the balance to pinot noir. The winery has added

a traditional but modernly appointed barrel-aging cave and a new, technically advanced winemaking facility to support these important wines. Additionally, all of the winery's farming follows sustainable techniques to ensure the best-quality grapes with the gentlest footprint on this land.

Above: Modern in style, a traditional barrel-aging cave stores Hanzell Vineyards wines.
Photograph by M.J. Wickham

Facing Page: The Hanzell Vineyards wine library is a perfect setting to share a glass.
Photograph by M.J. Wickham

Previous Pages: Hanzell Vineyards' de Brye Vineyard was planted in 1976.
Photograph by M.J. Wickham

Today Hanzell Vineyards has a primary goal of producing the high-class wines in an attempt not to mimic France but rather to compete by carrying out Zellerbach's vision. Fifty years in California's winemaking history is the equivalent of centuries in the Old World. With many more years to come, Hanzell Vineyards will prove itself dedicated to the legacy of the Ambassador's estate through the reverence of winemaking tradition and the thoughtful advancement of winemaking practices.

WINE & FARE

Hanzell Vineyards Chardonnay

Pair with Dover Sole Véronique, fingerling potatoes, fennel, celery verjus sauce with grapes—Chef Zach Bell, Café Boulud Palm Beach.

Hanzell Vineyards Pinot Noir

Pair with boneless rack of venison or lamb, glazed chestnuts, forest mushrooms, Oregon huckleberry sauce—Chef Andrew Cain, Santé at The Fairmont Sonoma Mission Inn & Spa.

Tastings
Open by appointment only

Hartford Family Winery

Forestville

About 15 miles from the Pacific Ocean, Hartford Family Winery rests comfortably just west of the small town of Forestville in the Green Valley of Russian River Valley Appellation. The winery focuses on single vineyards, compelled by their challenging geography, producing only meager amounts of exceptionally expressive grapes. Family-owned since 1993, the winery sources fruit from some of the best known cool-climate wine-growing regions—Green Valley, Russian River Valley, Los Carneros, Anderson Valley and the "true" Sonoma Coast—to craft small lots of elegant wines with passion and personality.

Hartford Family Winery released its first vintage—1994—to great acclaim. Within two years, Hartford Court wines were noted across several prestigious publications. This success stems from a singular mission: The winery embraces a wine-growing philosophy that equates a high-risk approach to achieve high rewards. Seeking out difficult and marginal vineyard sites for its bottlings, the team believes that some of the most challenging places to grow wine grapes often produce wines of the greatest character.

Hartford Family Winery's objective is to search out and develop vineyards that will not only provide complex flavor profiles, but that also possess a true sense of place. The winery's vineyards, by virtue of their sites, display characteristics that are distinctive and appear as a common thread from vintage to vintage. Through two distinct labels, the winery crafts some 18 different wines each vintage. The Hartford Court label features small lots of distinctive pinot noirs and chardonnays, while the Hartford label is reserved for the winery's old-vine, Russian River Valley zinfandels.

Top Left: Hartford Family Winery makes its home in Forestville, California.
Photograph by Hartford Family Winery

Bottom Left: The estate gardens are a great place for a casual stroll.
Photograph by M.J. Wickham

Facing Page: The vines absorb that sense of place.
Photograph by M.J. Wickham

The winery's number one goal is to make Hartford Court among the most compelling pinot noirs in the world, full of texture and wholly transparent in the expression of terroir. Hartford Court chardonnays are also carefully crafted from high-risk sites, showcasing complex and rich, multi-layered flavors and unmistakable aromas. Equally impressive is the fact that most of Hartford's zinfandel vineyards are more than a century old and are true treasures of wine country—producing bold and structured zinfandels with finesse, unlike any in the world.

Top Left: Proprietor Don Hartford spends some time with the barrels.
Photograph by M.J. Wickham

Bottom Left: Hartford offers a delightful sampling: Hartford Court Four Hearts Vineyards, Russian River Valley Chardonnay and Hartford Court Land's Edge Vineyards, Sonoma Coast Pinot Noir.
Photograph by Hartford Family Winery

Facing Page: The wine library offers an enticing selection.
Photograph by M.J. Wickham

Hartford Family Winery subscribes to the notion that great wines are made as a result of the skillful nurturing of great vineyards. Grapes are handpicked and hand sorted, see minimal intervention and are aged in 100-percent French oak barrels. The delicious wines are truly an expression of vineyard characteristics in their most authentic state.

HARTFORD
COURT

WINE & FARE

Hartford Court Four Hearts Vineyards, Russian River Valley Chardonnay
(100% chardonnay)

Pair with sautéed scallops, linguine and a light butter-cream sauce.

Hartford Court Land's Edge Vineyards, Sonoma Coast Pinot Noir
(100% pinot noir)

Pair with smoked duck breast and wild mushroom risotto.

Hartford Russian River Valley Zinfandel
(100% zinfandel)

Pair with bittersweet flourless chocolate cake.

Tastings
Open to the public daily, year-round

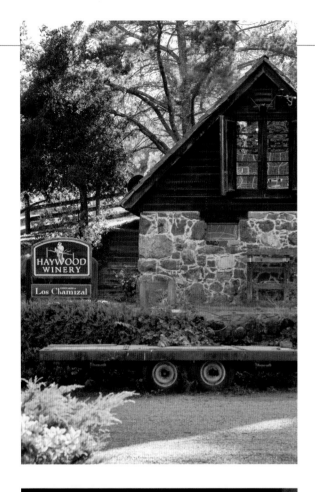

Haywood Estate

Sonoma

The hills beyond the historic town of Sonoma embrace a small valley called Chamizal where grape vines are planted on terraces carved from the rocky slopes. It was here in 1974 that Peter Haywood planted the vineyards that he named Los Chamizal, Spanish for the thickets of hardwood that covered the land. Soon he was sending to market different varietals that could adapt to the rugged terrain; but it was his zinfandel that captured most wine lovers' attention.

A bowl of carefully carved hillside terraces embraced by these hardwood thickets, Los Chamizal is the sinuous co-creation of Peter and nature, the birth of an exemplary wine-country landscape. The soil is thin and rocky; the solar exposure, full and intense; the nighttime breezes from nearby San Francisco Bay, a cooling balm for what is today recognized as one of the classic zinfandel vineyards in all of California.

With plantings grafted from a wide range of pre-Prohibition vines, exacting and sparse regimens of water and natural fertilizers and skilled cultivation and harvest by hand, the grapes grown here make some of the most elegant and refined zinfandels anywhere.

Top Left: Previously a stable, the Haywood office has been transformed into an idyllic setting for the development of the wine program.
Photograph by M.J. Wickham

Bottom Left: Peter and Maggie Haywood take a break on the porch of the cabin where they live. This is true wine-country living.
Photograph by M.J. Wickham

Facing Page: The Haywood vineyards roll over a rocky terrace. The soil here defines the flavors ensuring uniqueness in every bottle.
Photograph by M.J. Wickham

Of the 280 acres of land, 90 are planted to vines. In general, the soils of Los Chamizal are shallow—six inches to two feet—and poor, ranging from fractured red rock to volcanic tuft soil. The low nutrient levels contribute to the character of the wines by restricting growth and leaf production. The breezes off the mountain and from nearby San Francisco Bay keep the days temperate and nights cool.

Rocky Terrace Zinfandel is a sloping eight-acre block that faces south and turns southeast as it descends from 800 feet to 600 feet in elevation. This zinfandel is made from the fruit of a single block deeply rooted in fractured basalt, open to late afternoon sun. Rich in red fruit and structure without being heavy or jammy, 15-year-old Rocky Terrace remains full of fruit and complexity to this day.

Morning Sun Zinfandel wines are softer, yet nuanced and memorable. This zinfandel makes up a five-acre block on a distinct rise of land on the eastern side of the valley. The soil is sandy loam about two to two-and-a-half feet deep, and the site slopes downward from 350 feet to 250 feet elevation directly toward the rising sun. They shine with a brightness born of a single block of gnarled vines basking in the fog-filtered rays of the early sun.

Top Left: At the stone house terrace, the vineyards are a great view.
Photograph by M.J. Wickham

Middle Left: The main reservoir offers a quiet spot for picnicking.
Photograph by M.J. Wickham

Bottom Left: The hillside vineyards are carved from the nearby slopes.
Photograph by M.J. Wickham

Facing Page: Haywood offers an array of wonderful zinfandel wine.
Photograph by M.J. Wickham

Los Chamizal Zinfandel is a mirror for the entire Haywood Estate. A blend of nine distinctly different zinfandel blocks, this wine is a well-integrated reflection of the estate's characteristic flavors of pepper, spice and black fruit.

Gazing over the unparalleled beauty of this vineyard while sipping these smooth and polished products of its fruit, one can't help but marvel at the wonder of it all, a single harmony conspired somehow by man and nature.

WINE & FARE

Morning Sun Zinfandel

*Pair with roasted venison cooked with garlic cloves,
extra virgin olive oil and smoky bacon.*

Rocky Terrace Zinfandel

*Pair with borscht and beef brisket with sautéed apples.
For the summer, try pairing with barbecue-flavored dishes.*

Los Chamizal Zinfandel

*Pair with jambalaya and spicy sausage
or hoppin' john with hambone.*

Tastings
Open by appointment only

Hughes Family Vineyards

Sonoma

One essential element in making quality wines—besides, of course, superior grapes—is attention to detail. To achieve the highest possible quality in its wines, Hughes Family Vineyards was founded on the principle of carefully attending to each step of the winemaking process, from the vine to the wine. The winery nurtures the grapes in its certified-organic vineyards so that the highest-quality fruit is used to produce remarkable wines. Personal attention to every detail ensures that the estate's unique terroir is taken to its fullest potential, resulting in wines that speak from the earth, from Sonoma's fascinating wine country.

Keith and Cherie Hughes come from very different fields than winemaking, but their shared passion for the wine business is evident in the glass. Originally from Dallas, the two decided to pursue their dream to return to California, Keith leaving a position as chairman and CEO of Associates First Capital, and Cherie leaving a career as a doctor of clinical psychology. The foothills of Sonoma posed a stark change in landscape, and here, in 2001, the couple purchased two young, organic vineyards in Glen Ellen. They manage the winery together, with Keith overseeing the vineyards, and Cherie handling most of the thinking. And for the two, the partnership and challenges could not be more appealing.

Top Left: Keith and Cherie Hughes, founders and proprietors of Hughes Family Vineyards, stand in their Savannah Vineyard.
Photograph by M.J. Wickham

Bottom Left: The Hughes family offers a private wine tasting at the estate.
Photograph by M.J. Wickham

Facing Page: The Wild Turkey and Savannah Vineyards are situated in the foothills of the Mayacamas.
Photograph by M.J. Wickham

The site of the vineyards is certainly unique, nestled on a hillside overlooking the majestic Mayacamas Mountains and surrounded by ancient oaks. With a microclimate of warm, sunny days and late afternoons cooled by maritime breezes, the fruit develops with only nature's touch—all of the farming practices are organic.

In 2003 the Hughes developed a friendship with award-winning winemaker Kerry Damskey who believes as they do that winemaking is an art as well as a science. As winemaker for Hughes Family Vineyards, Kerry brings a certain wizardry to his techniques as he creates full-bodied wines that are an expression of the land and the grapes' identity.

Recently the Hughes partnered with Damskey to open Terroirs Artisan Wines in Geyserville. Here the Hughes' highly acclaimed syrah and zinfandel wines can be tasted. While Hughes Family Vineyards has focused on the production of remarkable zinfandel and syrah varietals, the winery recently added a rosé to its repertoire, along with sachets of fresh lavender from their lavender gardens as well as their intensely flavorful, organic, cold-pressed olive oil.

Top Left: Tuscan style meets modern architecture at Hughes Family Vineyards.
Photograph by M.J. Wickham

Bottom Left: The stars and moonlight welcome evening guests.
Photograph by M.J. Wickham

Facing Page: The private estate tasting room overlooks the Wild Turkey Vineyard.
Photograph by M.J. Wickham

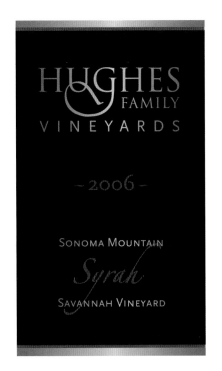

Farming organically since inception, Hughes Family Vineyards grows what it grows so that the best is produced in every way. As each vintage is released, Keith and Cherie come closer and closer to achieving near-perfect representations of their unique locale, which is fundamentally what we are asking for in a Hughes Family wine.

WINE & FARE

Hughes Family Vineyards Zinfandel
(100% zinfandel from the Wild Turkey Vineyard)

Pair with pasta with red sauce—the spicier the better—and grilled steaks, chops and burgers.

Hughes Family Vineyards Syrah
(100% syrah from the Savannah Vineyard)

Pair with duck breast on a warm spinach salad, roasted pork loin with cranberry-ginger chutney, or roast turkey.

Hughes Family Vineyards Syrah Rosé
(100% syrah from the Savannah Vineyard)

Pair with a warm afternoon, good friends, some salty Maracoma almonds and a little artisan cheese.

Tastings
Available at Terroirs Artisan Wines
Open to the public daily, seasonally

Imagery Estate Winery

Glen Ellen

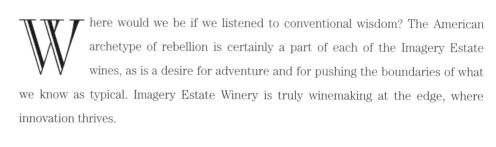

Where would we be if we listened to conventional wisdom? The American archetype of rebellion is certainly a part of each of the Imagery Estate wines, as is a desire for adventure and for pushing the boundaries of what we know as typical. Imagery Estate Winery is truly winemaking at the edge, where innovation thrives.

In 1983 Joe Benziger came to Sonoma where he worked with his family to establish Benziger Family Winery. While working there, Joe seized an opportunity to spotlight some unusual grape varietals that traditionally had been blended into single varietal wines. With skill and passion, Joe vinified these special lots into a series of wines he labeled Imagery Estate. Joe's experimentation with unusual and underappreciated grapes continues today, and he has added several innovative blends as well. For example, viognier, a nearly unheard of varietal in the Sonoma region, is now made as a powerful yet floral white wine. Lagrein, an even rarer varietal originating in Northern Italy, is vinified into a robust red wine that pairs nicely with food. These limited-production wines are a perfect escape from the ordinary.

Top Left: In Imagery Estate Winery's tasting room, guests can always expect the unexpected.
Photograph by M.J. Wickham

Middle Left: The Parthenon appears—overtly, obliquely or in the shadows—in each of the specially commissioned works of art featured on Imagery labels.
Photograph by M.J. Wickham

Bottom Left: The Sunny Slope vineyard is beautiful, bountiful and certified Biodynamic.
Photograph by M.J. Wickham

Facing Page: Raise a glass, add a bit of sunshine, and enjoy the afternoon on one of the beautiful terraces.
Photograph by M.J. Wickham

In the early days, as the first lots of Imagery Estate wines were fermenting, Joe met renowned local artist Bob Nugent through happenstance—the two found themselves playing a round of golf at a local course. A shared passion for wine and art proved fruitful, and soon the pair found a creative way to fuse art and wine at Imagery. Today each and every one of Imagery's wines features a new work of art on its label, and the original artwork hangs in Imagery's gallery. Bob Nugent continues to curate a collection of more than 200 pieces of art from some of the most notable contemporary artists working today.

Top Left: Rare, sophisticated and sometimes overlooked varietals make up Imagery's artistic palate—think whites, reds and out-of-the-ordinary.
Photograph by M.J. Wickham

Bottom Left: In the heart of the Sonoma Valley, Imagery Estate Winery has wines that pair well with nature's splendor.
Photograph by M.J. Wickham

Facing Page: Take in Imagery's artwork collection of more than 200 pieces commissioned from among the world's most notable contemporary artists, on permanent display in the gallery and tasting room.
Photograph by M.J. Wickham

And the wines? Wow oui! Over the last decade, Imagery's thirst for experimentation and willingness to do things the hard way led the winery to embrace Biodynamic farming on its 20-acre estate. An advanced form of organic farming, Biodynamics uses a holistic approach that enhances the individuality and uniqueness of a vineyard. Imagery is nothing if not distinctive, and that's the way Joe likes it. The paradigm of winemaking is shifting, and Imagery is at the forefront of that movement.

IMAGERY
ESTATE WINERY

WINE & FARE

Imagery White Burgundy
(56% chardonnay, 28% pinot blanc, 16% pinot meunier)
Pair with salmon in lemon butter sauce.

Imagery Grenache
Pair with roasted pork loin with sage and rosemary.

Imagery Tempranillo
Pair with grilled short ribs.

Tastings
Open to the public daily, year-round

Iron Horse Vineyards

Sebastopol

In 1985 Ronald Reagan sat down with Mikhail Gorbachev in the first of four summit meetings that would lead to the fall of the Soviet Union and the end of the Cold War. What better way to bring down walls than with a glass of top-quality sparkling wine. At that table, Iron Horse wine reported for duty, and for the subsequent presidential administrations, Iron Horse became the go-to bottle for White House bubbly. It is no wonder then that Iron Horse is considered an icon in the American marketplace.

Iron Horse Vineyards may be hard to get to—well off the beaten path in Green Valley in the coolest, foggiest part of the Russian River Valley, 13 miles from the Pacific—but the reward for finding this stunning location is phenomenal. In fact, the virtual stumbled-upon nature of the site could take credit for its purchase in 1976 by Audrey and Barry Sterling, who, certain they were lost, stumbled upon the brilliant land—a sort of grapey Camelot in the rolling hills of Sonoma.

There were 110 acres in vine at the time, originally planted by Forrest Tancer when he was working for Rodney Strong. Forrest and the Sterlings became partners, upgraded the vineyard, engineered an elaborate frost protection system and built the winery. During the leveling of ground they unearthed a horse-topped weathervane, which became the winery's logo; the name Iron Horse came from a train that stopped at Ross Station at the turn of the 20th century. The winery officially opened in 1979—coincidentally on Barry's 50th birthday—with the first vintage of estate pinot noir; the first vintage for the sparkling wines came out in 1980.

Top Left: Three generations of Sterlings live on the property, ranging in age from 14 to 80. Laurence Sterling is Director of Operations, overseeing the vineyards.
Photograph by M.J. Wickham

Bottom Left: A sparkling combination: A glass of bubbly meets cherry tomatoes stuffed with goat cheese and garnished with chive flowers—all grown on the estate.
Photograph by M.J. Wickham

Facing Page: Iron Horse is 300 acres of gently rolling hills, covered in vines. Just the lay of the land will make you fall in love with the place.
Photograph by M.J. Wickham

Iron Horse is truly a family affair. Audrey and Barry's daughter, Joy Sterling, joined the winery in 1985 and has since become the face of Iron Horse. The Sterlings' son Laurence, his wife Terry and their children moved to Iron Horse in 1990 and built their home on the far southwest corner of the property. And though Audrey and Barry are retired, they still reside at the heart of the property in the original Victorian home built in 1876.

Above: Iron Horse's architectural style is called Sonoma rustic elegance at its best.
Photograph by M.J. Wickham

Facing Page Top: The vineyard is broken down into small, individual blocks, tightly delineated by the changes in elevation, slope, the aspect of the sun, soil shifts and how the fog settles. Known as "Q," this is one of the family's favorite sites for pinot noir.
Photograph by M.J. Wickham

Facing Page Bottom Left: Iron Horse is sustainably farmed. All of the farming decisions are made on a vine-by-vine basis.
Photograph by M.J. Wickham

Facing Page Bottom Right: Besides the vineyards, co-founder Barry Sterling grows all kinds of fruit and vegetables, including hundreds of pumpkins for the fall.
Photograph by M.J. Wickham

The winery's viticultural knowledge has advanced light years from the original 110 acres that were planted in 1970. What was once one block is now broken down into five, further honing in on the estate's distinct characteristics—each being planted with specific rootstock, clonal selections, trellising, even occasional changes in row direction, with the goal of pulling more distinctive flavors out of the ground.

As well, Iron Horse is finding itself pushing a new slogan: Eat, drink and be green. Making the transition to clean energy is essential for the future of our world, and Iron Horse finds itself a lead proponent in the movement. Engaged in precision farming, Iron Horse performs under the guidance of the current leading viticultural expert. The Iron Horse family is a highly acclaimed pioneer of Green Valley within the Russian River area of Sonoma County.

The Iron Horse concept is to make estate-bottled wines, which show a definite sense of place. The family feels very strongly about making wines that are specific to the Green Valley appellation, through their special vineyard and the vintage, making the best wines of the year, and never falling back on "recipe" winemaking.

Above Left: The impressive entrance to the winery is called Palm–Olive Drive, for the alternating palm and olive trees planted over 30 years ago.
Photograph by M.J. Wickham

Above Right: Iron Horse is renowned for gracious entertaining, with dinner parties for hundreds of guests seated at one long table.
Photograph by M.J. Wickham

Facing Page: Winery CEO Joy Sterling offers a toast to friends and family.
Photograph by M.J. Wickham

The wines are expressive, stylish, highly nuanced, bright, focused, soft and silky. They exude quality and class. Above all, the winery strives for exquisite balance in its wines. Preferring, they say, not to knock but rather glide your socks off.

IRON HORSE™
VINEYARDS

WINE & FARE

Iron Horse 2005 Wedding Cuvée
(87% pinot noir, 13% chardonnay)

Pair with halibut wrapped with prosciutto and rosemary, served with black olive tapenade.

Iron Horse 1996 Blanc de Blancs LD
(100% chardonnay)

Pair with Harris crab with raw asparagus and shaved-shallot salad, olive oil and fried Meyer lemons.

Iron Horse 2006 Estate Chardonnay
(100% chardonnay)

Pair with baby onion, smokey bacon and Teleme cheese tarts.

Tastings
Open to the public daily, year-round

J. Rochioli
Vineyard and Winery

Healdsburg

J oe Rochioli has certainly led an interesting life. At eight years old, he was barreling through the dusty streets in a Model T, perhaps to the panic of pedestrians, but it was certainly a different time then. These were the days of the Old Timers, when subsistence was based on doing it yourself—if something was broken, you fixed it or it stayed broken. These were also the early days of American winemaking, when the idea of vineyard designation was unheard of; most of the wine ended up in the same barrel. The farms then were toiled by migrant workers with machetes. Nowadays, when many wineries are fueled with suits and high blood pressure, Joe is certainly a rarity.

From a family of grape-growers, Joe spent the mid part of the 20th century developing a reputation for unparalleled fruit, supplying for a slew of wineries. In 1938 Joe's father had purchased the Rochioli farm that would soon pass to his son. Joe and his father, Joe Sr., planted the first of the varietals, sauvignon blanc, in 1959; but Joe wanted to plant little French clones here, an idea that was nearly considered laughable, making the clones hard to find. Not until '68 did he gets his hands on some, setting a precedent of determination to not only survive in the blossoming industry, but to settle for nothing less than the best in the world. The climate proved ideal for pinot noir, chardonnay and sauvignon blanc, and his grape list of wineries grew exponentially.

Top Left: At the entry to the winery and tasting room, there is a promise of good things to come.
Photograph by M.J. Wickham

Bottom Left: From the picnic area, the Russian River Valley floor offers great views.
Photograph by M.J. Wickham

Facing Page: The Estate Sweetwater Vineyard is the highest elevation on the property.
Photograph by M.J. Wickham

Top: The entry and picnic area are perfect spots to look out over the Russian River Valley.
Photograph by M.J. Wickham

Bottom: The tasting room offers a few estate wines from which to choose.
Photograph by M.J. Wickham

Top: The family Model T truck has been on the property since the 1930s.
Photograph by M.J. Wickham

Bottom: Joe and Tom Rochioli spend some time on the property.
Photograph by M.J. Wickham

Joe's son, Tom Rochioli, found himself ready to get out of corporate America. He brought to his father a program to develop the successful grape-growing business into a winery. In 1982 he became a partner. Joe still runs the vineyards, while Tom handles the winery itself. They brought some of that old-fashioned method to their new partnership; they even designed the winery buildings and helped build the winery themselves. Producing fruit from those same clones planted in the '60s, the Rochiolis call first dibs on the harvest, selling the rest to a variety of wineries. By keeping its own wine production low, quality stays high, and the result is that the winery sells out of everything it makes.

The winery is located in an idyllic spot with views out to a rose garden and the rolling, hillside vineyards. Tom and Joe took great strides to develop a place that is elegant yet modest. There is even an art gallery that features a revolving collection of work by local Sonoma County artists. But it is in the vineyards where the Rochiolis developed an intimate knowledge of the soil and climate variation. Divided into distinctive blocks, the vineyards feature numerous clones from which to pull their wines. Each of these blocks displays its unique terroir. The variety of soils here works wonders if you just know how to treat each one. The Rochiolis played a major role in establishing the Russian River Valley as a petite Côte d'Or with terroir-driven wines.

Left: The old horse barn was built in 1889.
Photograph by M.J. Wickham

Facing Page: The Estate Chardonnay vineyard has the rolling hills of the Russian River Valley in the background.
Photograph by M.J. Wickham

Wine is the family tradition for the Rochiolis—once a month, their large family gathers for lively conversation, great wine and a savory home-cooked meal. And as the family comes and goes, Joe continues to stay productive. He spends his time restoring antique cars—including a Model T and ranch artifacts like a late 19th-century outhouse. Joe does what he does for the challenge, not the pay. And if there is anything a look at his cache of antique weapons would reveal, it is that Joe sticks to his guns. J. Rochioli Vineyards and Winery is about maintaining a good family relationship, and even more about the old-fashioned way of doing things.

2007

ROCHIOLI

RUSSIAN RIVER VALLEY

Pinot Noir

ESTATE GROWN

WINE & FARE

Estate Sauvignon Blanc
Pair with lightly spiced ceviche or oysters.

Estate Chardonnay
Pair with bacon-wrapped scallops.

Estate Pinot Noir
Pair with roasted pork loin with garlic and rosemary.

Tastings
Open to the public Thursday through Monday and by appointment only Tuesday and Wednesday

Jacuzzi Family Vineyards

Sonoma

Giovanni and Teresa Jacuzzi raised seven sons and six daughters in Casarsa, Italy. Giovanni grew grapes for winemaking, worked as a furniture maker, and operated the newsstand at the town's railway station. In 1907 two of his sons traveled to America to live the dream. Through the next few years, three of their brothers joined them to set up a woodworking and machine shop named Jacuzzi Brothers, Inc. in Berkeley, California. Brother Rachele was an inventor in the field of fluid dynamics and hydromechanics and designed a very lightweight and fast propeller called The Jacuzzi Toothpick. During WWI an aircraft engine manufacturer learned of the Jacuzzi Brothers' inventions and asked them to manufacture propellers for the U.S. Army Air Corps. The propeller now hangs in the Smithsonian Institute's Aviation and Space Museum.

In December 1920 the remaining family—Giovanni, Teresa, their children, daughter-in-law and first grandchild—emigrated to America. The Jacuzzi Brothers continued their inventions, and in 1921 the first fully enclosed cabin monoplane was developed, which carried eight people at 120 miles per hour, a very efficient design, and with which the brothers won the rights to fly mail, freight and passengers from historic Gilman Field in Berkeley to the airstrip at the base of El Capitan in Yosemite Valley. On the return of the inaugural flight, the pilot buzzed his girlfriend over Modesto and unfortunately crashed the airplane, killing one of the seven brothers. Giovanni and Teresa persuaded their sons that maybe there was a safer business.

Top Left: Guests can enjoy lunch in the grand piazza.
Photograph by M.J. Wickham

Bottom Left: The Italian stone cast fountain of Neptune overlooks the winery and vineyards.
Photograph by M.J. Wickham

Facing Page: The grand piazza radiates the wine-country aesthetic.
Photograph by M.J. Wickham

Successive inventions included the propeller-based frost machines for citrus groves and vineyards, wine filters for the wine industry, and in 1926 the gold medal-winning Jacuzzi injector pump, which was the most efficient way to pump water. Jacuzzi became one of the largest manufacturers of water pumps in the world, and in the mid-1940s a home-therapy pool was designed for one of the brothers' sons who had rheumatoid arthritis.

Today Jacuzzi Family Vineyards, located in the famous Sonoma-Carneros region, is one of the first wineries one encounters when visiting wine country. The winery offers complimentary tastings of a wide range of Italian varieties, including the more well-known sangiovese, barbera, primitivo, pinot grigio and moscato alongside unique and difficult-to-find varieties such as arneis, lagrein, nebbiolo and nero d'Avola. The wines are true to their Italian counterparts despite the fact that the California climate and soils differ from those of Italy.

The winery, modeled after the family's home in the Friuli region of Italy, is a complex of smaller sand-colored, stone and stucco-clad structures organized around a romantic, central courtyard. Traditional architectural details and natural materials add to the visitor's sense that the buildings predate their actual construction. The interior features magnificent pieces of Italian art and handmade furnishings, among other exquisite artifacts.

Left & Facing Page: Jacuzzi Family Vineyards' winery is modeled after the family home in Italy.
Photographs by M.J. Wickham

Jacuzzi Family Vineyards is also home to The Olive Press, an award-winning producer of organic California extra virgin olive oil. A one-stop shop for "all things olive," it features a tasting bar, retail store and onsite olive-pressing production where visitors can watch olive oil being made.

Great Italian wines from the New World are now being brought to you by a family of generations dedicated to the art of discovery, food and wine.

WINE & FARE

Jacuzzi Family Vineyards Arneis

Pair with roasted halibut or sautéed veal cutlets flavored with olive oil, sage and lemon juice.

Jacuzzi Family Vineyards Sangiovese

Pair with sliced tomatoes or dishes with tomato sauces—spaghetti, pizza, stews.

Jacuzzi Family Vineyards Barbera

Pair with roasted prime ribs of beef and roasted potatoes.

Jacuzzi Family Vineyards Primitivo

Pair with game dishes, venison or wild boar, with cherry or blueberry sauce, or with earthy flavors such as mushrooms.

Tastings
Open to the public daily, year-round

Jordan Vineyard & Winery

Healdsburg

The Old World has a very distinct pleasure of the table that has often been lost in our modern society. Part of the job of a good winery today is to reinvigorate the masses with concepts of beautifully conceived menus with remarkable handcrafted wines. Jordan Vineyard & Winery serves as a steward of that tradition, one reminiscent of the great European wine estates of the 18th and 19th centuries. Year in and out, the Jordan winemaking team sets out to produce wines that enhance this food experience. And they do so with a deft hand.

Great wines, of course, are products of great vineyards. When Tom Jordan purchased several hundred acres of beautiful Sonoma County land in the early 1970s, fine wine in California was still in its formative years. Tom saw this era as a great opportunity to produce wine in the old style, designed specifically to go with a meal, never to overshadow it. The winemakers toiled over the land, discovering its potential for growing cabernet sauvignon, merlot and chardonnay. Stretched over Alexander Valley and Russian River Valley, Jordan's vineyards are maintained in the fashion befitting the smaller, family-owned winery that Jordan is—with the preservation of integrity.

Because Jordan sees wine in the broader context—as not merely a freestanding beverage, but as an extension of the meal—its winemaking team and vineyard staff continually work to make the best possible product. This begins naturally with the wine itself, mastering Old World artistry while utilizing New World technology—handpicking parallels more state-of-the-art techniques like pneumatic presses and temperature-controlled fermenting tanks.

Top Left: *Bacchus, the Roman God of Wine* was purchased by Tom Jordan in 1987 and was originally created by Jacopo Sansovino in 1511 A.D. The sculpture now sits in the winery courtyard.
Photograph by M.J. Wickham

Bottom Left: Nestled among the rolling hills of Alexander Valley in Sonoma, Jordan Vineyard & Winery offers a picturesque setting including grapevines, olive trees, vegetable gardens and the serene Jordan Lake.
Photograph by M.J. Wickham

Facing Page: The 1,500-acre Jordan Winery in Alexander Valley is modeled after an 18th-century French estate.
Photograph by M.J. Wickham

Jordan's first cabernet sauvignon in 1976 was crafted under the legendary André Tchelistcheff, who in those early years had Rob Davis, Jordan's winemaker, by his side. Along with many of the original workers for the first vintage, the winemaking team strives for the suppleness and delicacy that has given Jordan its reputation.

The experience of the wine is also vital. Much of the draw to Jordan is the winery itself. The 18th-century, French château-inspired winery's hilltop location is ideal for soaking in some of those fascinating wine-country vistas. The Jordan estate is a landscaping marvel; French organic gardens surround the winery, with poplars and sycamores and plenty of fruits and vegetables for sampling; seasonal recipes are developed by Jordan's executive chef Todd Knoll, a private dining room and guest suites are inside, while a magnificent terrace is the perfect spot for outdoor entertaining. Each amenity demonstrates Jordan's philosophy: to provide the ultimate guest experience in Sonoma.

Top Left: In the elegant dining room at Jordan Vineyard & Winery, guests can enjoy delicious meals prepared by executive chef Todd Knoll.
Photograph by Caitlin McCaffrey

Bottom Left: Luxury accommodations represent the best in wine-country living.
Photograph by M.J. Wickham

Facing Page: The oak tank room at Jordan Winery holds the original 21 tanks that were installed in 1976.
Photograph by M.J. Wickham

Above Top: CEO John Jordan now leads the family business and continues his father's vision of producing memorable wines that complement your life experiences.
Photograph by Dino Publishing

Above Bottom: Winemaker Rob Davis has been with the winery since the very first vintage of 1976 and maintains the Jordan philosophy of making food-friendly wines.
Photograph by M.J. Wickham

Left: Whether they come for the wines or the tour, guests find that it is the ultimate wine-country experience in Sonoma County.
Photograph by M.J. Wickham

At Jordan, the idea that wines should be an accompaniment to everyday life experiences holds true. The wines are specifically made to complement food; some of the winemaker favorites are scallops with the crisp chardonnay or lamb with the cabernet.

Tours and tastings are Jordan's specialty, whether guests meander the gardens or take a behind-the-scenes look into the winemaking facility. When visiting the winery, guests experience wine country at its best—and the day is always memorable.

One of the great benefits of owning 1,600 acres of woodlands is having the ability to branch out with agriculture. Since 1999 Jordan has produced its own olive oil. Though it is developed over a protracted process, the olive oil that comes from Jordan is unmatched and well worth the effort. Along with the olive oil, Jordan creates its own preserves, honey

and hearth breads, any of which can be sampled in the dining room, beneath the 17th-century Louis XIII walnut cartouche.

A producer of some 90,000 cases of wine a year, Jordan Vineyard & Winery is always abuzz with anticipation. Harvest is an electrifying spell. Each year during harvest the staff puts together a savory lunch—a veritable feast for the fall; and everyone shows up to take part in the excitement. This is part of the wonder of winemaking, celebrating the question, "What will this vintage bring?"

Above: The cellar room at Jordan Winery offers guests the opportunity to taste current releases and library wines.
Photograph by M.J. Wickham

Facing Page: Jordan Vineyard & Winery chardonnay and cabernet sauvignon are on display.
Photograph by Kelly McManus

Through a deep understanding of the land combined with skilled artisans and an estate-wide fight for integrity, family-owned Jordan Vineyard & Winery is a rare exception to the massive consolidation in the wine industry. *Wine & Spirits* labels Jordan's as the most-requested cabernet sauvignon in white-tablecloth restaurants across the country. Jordan is not carving out a niche in California winemaking—it merely tries to change the way we live. And it appears to be working.

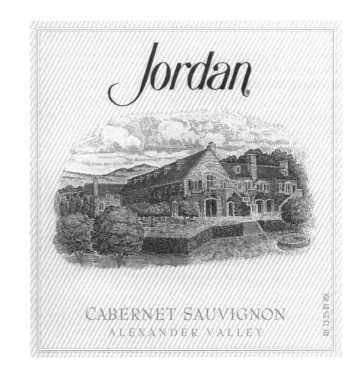

WINE & FARE

Jordan Chardonnay, Russian River Valley
(100% chardonnay)

Pair with braised artichoke appetizer, wine-country style.

Jordan Cabernet Sauvignon, Alexander Valley
(76% cabernet sauvignon, 18% merlot, 4% petit verdot, 2% cabernet franc)

Pair with braised beef maître menan.

Tastings
Open by appointment only

Keller Estate
Winery & Vineyards

Petaluma

Magnificent Keller Estate Winery, in the Sonoma Coast/Petaluma Gap appellation, looms formidably, surrounded by vineyard-covered rolling hills and picturesque viewpoints where one is treated to astonishingly beautiful vistas of the Keller property and surroundings. Family owned and operated, Keller Estate has historical origins that are intriguing and almost serendipitous, combining European ancestry with Hispanic culture, passion and a dash of luck.

The surname Keller is Swiss-German and means "cellar," the underground place where, for centuries, beer and wine were stored below the typical European home. Indeed, the family crest appears on the Keller Estate label with its focal point being the key of the cellar. The legacy began very early in the 20th century when the family patriarch, Wilhem Alexander Keller, left his native Switzerland journeying to Mexico to build that country's first hydroelectric plant. There he fell in love with both the land and a lady, settled down, had a family and stayed. Arturo Keller, founder of Keller Estate, is Wilhem's grandson. Born and raised in Mexico, Arturo also studied civil engineering, married, raised a family, and developed his outstanding and continuing professional career there. Arturo first came to the San Francisco Bay Area in 1977. The area so captivated him that he returned continuously, acquiring property, and some years later met his wife Deborah. Together they often took road trips in his vintage cars, falling in love with Sonoma Coast and acquiring the land now comprising Keller Estate. They wanted to plant vineyards, essentially for their beauty as landscaping, and to create wine in small amounts as a hobby.

Top Left: Arturo and Deborah Keller are the founders and operators of Keller Estate.
Photograph courtesy of Keller Estate Winery & Vineyards

Middle Left: Chardonnay and pinot noir are the main focus for Keller Estate.
Photograph courtesy of Keller Estate Winery & Vineyards

Bottom Left: Ana Keller with her favorite chardonnay.
Photograph by Terry Hankins

Facing Page: La Cruz Vineyard offers a magnificent view.
Photograph by M.J. Wickham

At the time there were no existing vineyards in close proximity, so the future was uncertain. The now prestigious Sonoma Coast appellation was just budding. After some research and consulting with the University of California at Davis, the couple decided to plant chardonnay. The first vineyard was completed in 1989, followed by pinot noir plantings in '94 and '95. Each successive harvest confirmed excellent quality: Fruit born of the Keller land was consistently splendid, and the wine crafted from it worthy of bottling under the family name. This is exactly what Arturo's youngest daughter, Ana, proposed to do.

Since 1998 Ana Keller, a master in biopharmaceutical science, has joined Arturo in realizing a mutual dream: to grow, create and market the very highest quality fruit, and from it, make the finest wine the Keller land can bear. With Ana's participation, the vineyards expanded to 90 acres, greatly increasing pinot noir and adding many distinct clonal varieties. In 2000 Keller Estate proudly released its first vintage using the family name. The aspiration to build an enduring, multigenerational family enterprise took root.

The highest priority for the Kellers is to let the land dictate the winery practices; strict winemaking yields to the spirit of the fruit in guiding the wine's style. "This is the true art of winemaking," say Ana and Arturo. The Kellers' winemaker, Ross Cobb, agrees. Together they aim to perpetuate this legacy, so that 50 or 100 years from now, the terroir defining this property continues to shine on in the wines.

Top Left: A gentle breeze welcomes guests.
Photograph by M.J. Wickham

Middle Left: The façade of the winery stands the test of time.
Photograph by M.J. Wickham

Bottom Left: Keller Estate has mastered winemaking with style.
Photograph by M.J. Wickham

Facing Page: Guests enjoy the wines at the bar.
Photograph by M.J. Wickham

A visit to the winery perfectly illustrates the family's value for aesthetics and ancestry. The goal of family legacy not only drives winemaking decisions, but also is manifest in the winery building itself. Designed by world-renowned Mexican architect and family friend Ricardo Legorreta, the imposing structure housing the winery operations aligns beautifully with the California sunlight and Sonoma hills, conveying a strong sense of culture and timelessness. Local artwork, also featured throughout the winery, expresses the spirit of the geography in visual form, the perfect complement to the wonderful expression made through sense of taste: the wine. This is the fundamental philosophy of Keller Estate Winery & Vineyards—heritage is everything.

KELLER ESTATE

WINE & FARE

Oro de Plata Chardonnay
(100% chardonnay)

Pair with spicy Asian fusion cuisine, sautéed scallops, sushi and grilled fish.

La Cruz Vineyard Chardonnay
(100% chardonnay)

Pair with buttery sauces, lobster, creamy risotto, roasted chicken and crab cakes.

La Cruz Vineyard Pinot Noir
(100% pinot noir)

Pair with grilled salmon, roasted mushrooms, duck confit and herb-based preparations.

La Cruz Vineyard Syrah
(100% syrah)

Pair with roasted or grilled game, braised beef and rosemary-infused rack of lamb.

Tastings
Open by appointment only

Kendall–Jackson
Vineyard Estates

Santa Rosa

The proper location of vineyards is perhaps one of the single most important factors in creating world-class wines, and Kendall-Jackson, California's premier family-owned, environmentally friendly winery, recognized the importance of this concept very early in its history. Established in 1982, Kendall-Jackson's winemaking philosophy is to select fruit from its best vineyard estates, located on mountains, ridges, hillsides and benches, and to blend those special lots to deliver consistent quality and intense flavor from vintage to vintage. Though Kendall-Jackson produces wines from its Estate Vineyards located up and down the cool coast of California, it is in Sonoma County where founder and proprietor Jess Jackson has located Kendall-Jackson and made his home.

Jess spent nearly a decade developing his own wine style, for the importance of science and technology in the creation of world-class wines cannot be underestimated. Terroir, however—that mystical melding of light, water, soil, air and human touch—is considerably harder to define. The key to understanding terroir is to appreciate how the light, water, soil and climate of a given site interact with human contact to produce unique wines of exceptional quality. Tasting the distinctive wines made from Kendall-Jackson's mountain and hillside grapes goes a long way in defining terroir. The result of location can be tasted in Kendall-Jackson's Vintner's Reserve Chardonnay, a rich, round, flavorful wine made with handcrafted methods, including small oak barrel fermentation, malolactic fermentation and aging on the lees.

Though Kendall-Jackson's reputation has been built on the success of chardonnay, it is the red wine program that excites the winemakers. The Grand Reserve tier above Vintner's Reserve features dual or single appellation wines selected from the top

Top Left: The grape bins are a great place to see the vibrancy of the fruit.
Photograph courtesy of Kendall-Jackson Vineyard Estates

Bottom Left: Food and wine pairings at the Kendall-Jackson Wine Center get to the essence of the wine experience.
Photograph by M.J. Wickham

Facing Page: The view of Piner Hills Estate, Russian River Valley, is exceptional from any vantage point.
Photograph courtesy of Kendall-Jackson Vineyard Estates

three percent of the winery's estate grown grapes. Look for the Grand Reserve Cabernet Sauvignon, a perennial gold medal winner at the Sonoma County Harvest Fair.

For those wine lovers who are willing to try something special, there is Kendall-Jackson's Highland Estates series of wines. Eight single-vineyard, estate-grown wines give tasters a virtual tour of California's cool coastal vineyards stretching from Santa Barbara and Monterey counties, all the way up to Sonoma, Napa and Mendocino counties on the North Coast.

Located within Sonoma County are some spectacular mountain vineyards including Hawkeye Mountain, high above Alexander Valley, and Trace Ridge, in Knights Valley. Cool-climate Kendall-Jackson pinot noir is sourced from the Annapolis Estate vineyard on the Sonoma Coast and for merlot, Kendall-Jackson harvests from the cool hillsides of Taylor Peak in the Bennett Valley, south of Santa Rosa.

Kendall-Jackson is one of the few remaining California family-owned wineries of its size. Jess and his wife Barbara Banke continue to lead Kendall-Jackson into its next quarter century based on truth and wine integrity: Each bottle of Kendall-Jackson is as good as the last. In 2008 both the San Francisco International Wine Competition and *Wine & Spirits Magazine* proclaimed Kendall-Jackson Winery of the Year, fitting accolades for a winery celebrating nearly three decades of winemaking excellence.

Top Left: Winemaster Randy Ullom spends some time in his vineyards.
Photograph courtesy of Kendall-Jackson Vineyard Estates

Top Right: Jess Jackson and Robbie take a short break in the shade.
Photograph courtesy of Kendall-Jackson Vineyard Estates

Bottom: The Kendall-Jackson Wine Center in Santa Rosa is the wine-tasting hub for the winery.
Photograph by M.J. Wickham

Facing Page: The cool fog plays a heavy hand in the grape-growing process at Trace Ridge Estate, Knights Valley.
Photograph courtesy of Kendall-Jackson Vineyard Estates

Whether you are beginning or ending your Sonoma County wine tour, there are now two Kendall-Jackson tasting rooms to visit, each boasting a splendid array of wines and a knowledgeable staff eager to answer enological questions. Kendall-Jackson's original Wine Center & Gardens is located just off Highway 101 at the Fulton Road exit, north of Santa Rosa, and a cozy Kendall-Jackson tasting room awaits on the square in downtown Healdsburg. Both are centrally located for explorations of not only the Russian River Valley, but the Alexander and Dry Creek Valleys as well.

While the Healdsburg tasting room features the entire Kendall-Jackson wine lineup including the winery's upper-tier Highland Estates and Stature wines, visitors to the Wine Center can sample wine offerings from the Kendall-Jackson portfolio as well as indulge in a special food and wine Reserve tasting. Kendall-Jackson's Wine Center & Gardens has become one of wine country's top destinations. With its splendid château architecture and impeccable gardens, including a chef's sensory garden used exclusively by the Kendall-Jackson culinary team for education and research, the Kendall-Jackson Wine Center & Gardens is home to some of Sonoma County's best annual wine and food events. Tastings and tours are offered during the spring and summer months. This unique two-and-a-half acre garden is designed to educate and entertain wine connoisseurs who are looking to further their knowledge of the flavors and aromas found in wine. The annual Kendall-Jackson Heirloom Tomato Festival—a benefit for the School Garden Network—is held on the first Saturday after

Top & Middle Left: The Kendall-Jackson Wine Center is a pastoral château, sitting on 120 acres in Sonoma County. Hawkeye Mountain produces some of Kendall-Jackson's finest grapes.

Bottom Left & Facing Page: In winter, Hawkeye Mountain has incomparable terroir. At sunset, Sentinel Oak on the mountain embodies the spirit of California's wine country.

Previous Pages: The rolling hills of Hawkeye Mountain Estate, Alexander Valley, exemplify the terrain of Sonoma.
Photographs courtesy of Kendall-Jackson Vineyard Estates

Labor Day and features food and wine pairings utilizing the more than 175 heirloom tomato varieties grown in the Kendall-Jackson culinary garden. In addition to tomato tastings, there are cooking demonstrations and wine-education seminars, plenty of top Bay Area restaurants and live entertainment.

Growing grapes on the sides of mountains builds character—not only the character of the wine, but also the character of the people growing the grapes. It is not easy to grow grapes on mountains. Nor is it inexpensive. Patience and determination are required, along with sustainable farming practices and hard work. These are the key ingredients in maintaining a close, respectful relationship with nature.

WINE & FARE

Highland Estates
Seco Highlands Chardonnay
(100% chardonnay)

Pair with ginger crab cakes and baked brie with mushrooms and almonds.

Grand Reserve Pinot Noir
(100% pinot noir)

Pair with pan-roasted chicken breasts with black olive pesto.

Vintner's Reserve Cabernet Sauvignon
(96% cabernet sauvignon, 3% cabernet franc, 1% merlot)

Pair with rib-eye steaks with a soy and ginger marinade.

Stature Red Wine
(80% cabernet sauvignon, 10% cabernet franc, 5% merlot, 5% petit verdot)

Pair with baked fennel with gorgonzola.

Tastings
Open to the public daily, year-round

Lambert Bridge Winery

Healdsburg

Wine, at its basest, is a beverage; but for Lambert Bridge Winery, elegant wine at its greatest potential can be a bonding agent, a potent social mechanism through which experience of distinction in tastes can be shared. The mission is somewhat uncomplicated, funneled through a very welcoming standard: great wine served with great food shared by great friends. This philosophy comes from both the experiences and lifestyles of the individuals that make up the team, and the promise is in their aspiration to share their lifestyle with those who enjoy wine. The winery's European approach to life is paramount, for wine there is essential, part of the food, part of everyday life, rather than an occasional venture. The team certainly lives its credo; the family-owned winery, along with its winemakers, shares a passion to create wine that is individual, distinguished and unfailing through vintages.

Lambert Bridge Winery was built in 1975, making it one of the oldest wineries in Dry Creek since the days of Prohibition. The evolution of the winery begins with meticulous work in the vineyards, progressing with state-of-the-art berry-sorting techniques and some clear principles to elevate the wines to world-class status. Myriad educational and culinary events hosted year-round enhance the wine experience and make each visit much more than just a tasting.

Top Left: Vintage 1947 Fords welcome you to Lambert Bridge and remind you of the winery's deep roots and strong heritage in Dry Creek Valley.
Photograph by M.J. Wickham

Middle Left: The entrance to Lambert Bridge awakens your senses: a gateway to the ultimate wine-tasting experience.
Photograph by M.J. Wickham

Bottom Left: Lambert Bridge's hillside vineyards are home to prime fruit, where optimal growing conditions produce highly concentrated yields and wines of greater depth.
Photograph by M.J. Wickham

Facing Page: Personal attention is all yours in the rustically elegant Reserve Room, where an impressive lineup of limited-production wines aged in French oak are served in Riedel glassware under a vaulted redwood ceiling.
Photograph by M.J. Wickham

Above Top: Two Mugnaini wood-fired ovens anchor a popular culinary program that offers seasonal cooking classes with internationally acclaimed chefs and private winemaker dinners in the barrel room.
Photograph by M.J. Wickham

Above Middle: Hot, fresh pizzas are just one of the many culinary delights that Lambert Bridge guests enjoy at wine-club parties, seasonal outdoor activities and wine-blending classes with the winemakers.
Photograph by M.J. Wickham

Above Bottom: Gus, the winery dog and greeter, patrols the vineyards for turkeys and deer, ensuring perfect growing conditions for the grapes.
Photograph by M.J. Wickham

Left: Lambert Bridge's Mediterranean-style gardens are one of the many treasures you will find when you visit. Enjoy a picnic surrounded by beautiful landscapes and incredible views.
Photograph by M.J. Wickham

The European approach to winemaking dedicates itself to small lots of artisanal Bordeaux blends, crafting wines that enhance the everyday experience of drinking wine. This is Lambert Bridge's evolution, because everything changed under winemaker Jill Davis. With Mitch Firestone-Gillis at her side, Jill is credited with shifting the larger part of the winery's focus to these Bordeaux blends. However, Jill also brings this European styling to Dry Creek Valley's world-renowned reputation for world-class zinfandel. This approach has carved out a niche for Lambert Bridge Winery by producing zinfandels that are extraordinarily approachable and balanced, showing bright, fresh fruit from California's sunshine. "If you're going to do it," says Jill, "do it well." And she certainly does.

Right: French oak barrels are the backbone to Lambert Bridge's Bordeaux-blend program, adding beautiful flavors while maintaining an opulent, impeccable balance where the oak respects the fruit.
Photograph by M.J. Wickham

Facing Page Top: An expansive curly redwood bar fronted in hand-hammered copper welcomes you to the tasting room, where the trademark Lambert Bridge warmth and hospitality is served.
Photograph by M.J. Wickham

Facing Page Bottom Left: Single berry sorting, the last of a three-tier berry-sorting process, is one of the many detailed steps that differentiates Lambert Bridge and ensures that only the best grapes make it to the bottle.
Photograph by M.J. Wickham

Facing Page Bottom Right: The annual Harvest Festival in October celebrates the bounties of harvest with a traditional European feast and affirms the winery's culinary connection to the valley.
Photograph courtesy of Lambert Bridge Winery

Of course, everything starts in the vineyards. Having hillside vineyards means that some fruit does not ripen as quickly as others; so, multiple picks ensure uniform ripeness and flavor profiles. This is a standard of quality that is uncompromising. There is a certain comfort in this. Most visitors cannot find a Lambert Bridge wine they do not like, because the winery has set the hardnosed idea that everything must be world class.

A good way to see why the winery believes wine is so significant to our culture is by visiting. Creating a wine-country experience is of high priority, for the team is eager to share its lifestyle to all who come through the door. Warm, comfortable and inviting, the winery is tucked back under a grove of redwoods, with the building itself crafted mostly of redwood—a definitive California feel. Lush, expansive gardens animate the senses, but a tasting room visit reveals the lifestyles and passions of the winemakers; the visitor becomes part of the process, so that the winery's meticulous and rigid method of crafting is really seen. The welcoming tasting room is a friendly reflection of the home that the team has fashioned. Sipping a great Lambert Bridge cabernet in Riedel glassware, sampling a variety of fine local, handmade cheeses, artisanal breads and dried fruits, awakens the senses.

Above: Owning or managing 70 percent of its fruit sources, Lambert Bridge has mountainside vineyards, where the story begins with hard work and meticulous attention to detail.
Photograph by M.J. Wickham

Facing Page: Come warm up in the winter next to a roaring fireplace, or just stop in to immerse in a seasonal display of holiday decorations that is sure to make you feel at home.
Photograph courtesy of Lambert Bridge Winery

Food and friends are the crux of the Lambert Bridge process, perfectly embodied every October with the Harvest Celebration. This global tradition to celebrate the bounty is always a significant event at Lambert Bridge. Live music fills the air, while wood-fired ovens cook a huge feast that celebrates the pairing of local foods and artisanal wines, with, of course, great friends. Throughout the year, to reinforce this fundamental of food and wine coupling, Lambert Bridge Winery also offers a series of cooking courses, including The Art of Wood Fired Cooking with Chef Andrea Mugnaini. Cross the trestled bridge that bears its namesake, and enjoy their passion for sharing a wine-country lifestyle.

LAMBERT BRIDGE

WINE & FARE

Sonoma County Cabernet Sauvignon
(cabernet sauvignon, merlot, cabernet franc, petit verdot)

*Pair with filet mignon with red
wine-reduction mushroom sauce.*

Sonoma County Chardonnay
(chardonnay)

Pair with Meyer lemon-roasted chicken.

Sonoma County Petit Verdot
(petit verdot)

Pair with grilled leg of Sonoma lamb.

Tastings
Open to the public daily, year-round

Lancaster Estate

Healdsburg

Embarking on a remarkable career in the wine business in 1971, Ted Simpkins came to California in 1983 to pursue his dream of having his own winery. Several years after his arrival, he visited the former Maacama Creek Winery and knew this was where he wanted to develop a visionary project—focused on producing a great Bordeaux-style estate cabernet. Ted saw his dream come to fruition when this property became available in 1994; it was an ideal fit for his ambition. He named the estate Lancaster as a tribute to his family name.

Just over a decade after arriving in California, he made his first wine from this property in 1995 using fruit from the 20 acres of vineyards that existed on the 70-acre estate. He even expanded the plantings to 53 acres of Bordeaux varietals. Over the years, Ted built a core of talented people to run the winery that he had envisioned, opening in 2001 to critical acclaim. Ted, his wife, Nicole, and their twin daughters reside on the estate. The estate's co-proprietors' vision of creating world-class cabernet blends was about to be realized.

Top Left: Built in 2001, the winery was designed by Eugene Silva.
Photograph by M.J. Wickham

Middle Left: Sophia, Samantha and Nicole Simpkins enjoy a summer afternoon.
Photograph by M.J. Wickham

Bottom Left: The wine cave offers a unique dining experience.
Photograph by M.J. Wickham

Facing Page: The vineyards overlook the Mayacamas Mountains at the peak of Mt. St. Helena.
Photograph by M.J. Wickham

Lancaster Estate produces five wines, all anchored with a Bordeaux heritage. Over the 53 planted hillside acres, the winery grows the classic five Bordeaux varietals: cabernet sauvignon, merlot, malbec, petite verdot and cabernet franc. These red varietals are used as components for the Lancaster Estate Cabernet Sauvignon, the wonderfully soft and accessible red wine Sophia's Hillside Cuvee, the rich and densely concentrated Nicole's Proprietary Red, as well as an excellent cabernet sauvignon under the label Roth, which honors another family name. In addition to these four red wines, Lancaster Estate produces a limited-production sauvignon blanc called Samantha's, similar to the Sophia's Hillside Cuvee, both of which honor Ted and Nicole's daughters.

The winemaking at Lancaster Estate is under the guidance of Jennifer Higgins. Initially brought on as the assistant winemaker, Jennifer was promoted in 2004 to lead the winemaking team. Since then she has worked closely with consulting winemaker David Ramey to continue evolving the quality and expression of the wines from this hillside estate. The payoff has been apparent; Lancaster garnered top spots on *Wine Enthusiast*'s Top 100 Wines several years in a row, with high point ratings each time.

Right: Margaret looks over the vineyard.
Photograph by M.J. Wickham

Facing Page Top: The heart of the cave is a great place to start a tour.
Photograph by M.J. Wickham

Facing Page Bottom Left: The caves are an essential part of the wine-country experience.
Photograph by M.J. Wickham

Facing Page Bottom Right: The library tasting room has access reserved for members of the Lancaster Estate Wine Guild.
Photograph by M.J. Wickham

The estate itself is tucked into an angular southerly spur—truly a sub-appellation of the Alexander Valley, wedged between Knights Valley on the north and Chalk Hill on the south. The majority of the southeast-facing vineyards are situated on hillsides that were gently shaped by volcanic dust deposits. Planted exclusively to the five Bordeaux varietals, these steep hillsides, with rhyolitic soils, create a unique minerality and density in the estate's cabernet.

With a group of dedicated team members, the winery focuses on bringing the elements of the great site to its highest potential. Each year, the team refocuses its efforts on how to improve the results from the vineyard and the winemaking. "I believe today," says Ted, "that as stewards of this spectacular vineyard site, if we honor the character of our location and continue our dedication to making the highest quality of wines, no one else can replicate the wines that come from our estate.

We make our wines to honor the authenticity of our home and unique location." To experience this authenticity and uniqueness, visitors can enjoy a personal driving tour of the hillside vineyards, followed by intimate tastings in the wine caves.

Above Left: Carved deep into No Name Hill is the entry to the wine cave.
Photograph by M.J. Wickham

Above Top Right: The candle-lit entry into the cave guides the way to the barrels.
Photograph by M.J. Wickham

Above Bottom Right: A solid oak doorway leads into the cave.
Photograph by M.J. Wickham

Facing Page: A patchwork of merlot and cabernet vines rolls across the vineyards.
Photograph by M.J. Wickham

Well balanced and finely crafted, Lancaster Estate's wines are marked by incredible concentration and elegance. This push for quality establishes Lancaster Estate wines among the greats of California and, in time, one of the great wines of the world.

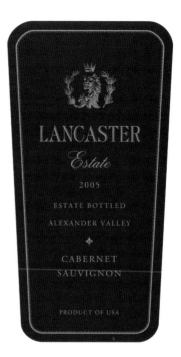

WINE & FARE

Lancaster Estate, "Estate Bottled"
Cabernet Sauvignon

Pair with braised beef short ribs and fresh herbs.

Lancaster Estate, "Sophia's"
Hillside Cuvee

Pair with pan-roasted Muscovy duck breast and slow-cooked Bing cherry sauce.

Lancaster Estate, "Nicole's"
Proprietary Red Blend

Pair with grilled local Sonoma CK lamb chops with seasonal root vegetables.

Lancaster Estate, "Samantha's"
Sauvignon Blanc

Pair with fresh Dungeness crab salad with avocado, grapefruit and sauvignon blanc verjus.

Tastings
Open by appointment only

Landmark Vineyards

Kenwood

A grape is a very fine agricultural product that requires great care. The hands that touch grapes, therefore, must develop a tradition of agricultural excellence. Landmark Vineyards grew out of a long history of that tradition. Since the mid-1800s, the name John Deere with the iconic green tractor has been the image of farming quality. And through this legacy, John Deere's descendants progress the family association through Landmark Vineyards. But the theme of merit does not end in the fields; rather, Landmark takes on the gargantuan task of enhancing the joy of daily living. And for this, wine country has undeniably taken notice.

Founded in 1974, Landmark Vineyards is a product of Damaris Deere Ford, John Deere's great-great-granddaughter. She founded the winery in Windsor but soon uprooted the winery for its current, bucolic setting in the heart of Sonoma Valley. Soon, Damaris encouraged her son, Michael Deere Colhoun, along with his wife, Mary, to take the reins of the budding winery. Michael and Mary equate Sonoma County to heaven. From this terrain, one of the world's best winemaking spots, the Colhouns seek a distinctive style statement, through which their ultra-premium wines are allowed to exemplify the terroir of Landmark's incredible geography.

Top Left: Proprietors of Landmark Vineyards Michael Deere Colhoun, great-great-great-grandson of John Deere, and his wife, Mary Colhoun, stand by one of the antique tractors on display at the winery.
Photograph by Ryan Lely

Bottom Left: The Overlook Chardonnay can be found on prestigious restaurant wine lists throughout the world.
Photograph by Kelly McManus

Facing Page: Landmark's verdant courtyard with its spectacular view of the Mayacamas Mountains is the perfect place to sip a glass.
Photograph by Robert Holmes

Landmark's winemaker, Eric Stern, pushes the Landmark principle of simply leaving wines alone, allowing the natural state to develop the flavor profile. Eric utilizes senses and aesthetics to generate balanced, full-flavored chardonnays and pinot noirs in the traditional Burgundian style. This is the art of winemaking at its finest. World-renowned enologist Helen Turley laid the foundation for Landmark's winemaking; the 1993 chardonnay, in fact, was the springboard of Landmark as an unstoppable winemaking force. The continual effort to perfect the winemaking craft fills Landmark's fine wines with great energy, and the wonderful style that has resulted is a testament to the winery's interpretation of vintages.

The winery itself sits right in the middle of the vineyards, and the good stewardship is evident on visit. With a guest cottage and tours on a horse-drawn wagon, the facility is geared toward that iconic, wine-country hospitality.

Top Left: Nestled at the foot of Sugarloaf State Park, Landmark Vineyards is a wine lover's dream, with award-winning wines, welcoming grounds and a bocce court.
Photograph courtesy of Landmark Vineyards

Middle Left: The spring cherry blossoms greet visitors of Landmark's tasting room.
Photograph courtesy of Landmark Vineyards

Bottom Left: Landmark's picnic grounds overlook the estate pond and vineyard.
Photograph by Rachel Capil

Facing Page: The gardens at Landmark Vineyards boast vibrant colors throughout the year.
Photograph by Rachel Capil

Through the winery, Landmark can fulfill its statement that begins with the critically acclaimed wines—Landmark wines have landed on *Wine Spectator*'s Top 100 multiple times over the last decade—but that extends well beyond. This is wine as an experience, and so the winery as a destination becomes an integral part of Landmark's philosophy: Wine, in its essence, boosts the daily component of gracious living.

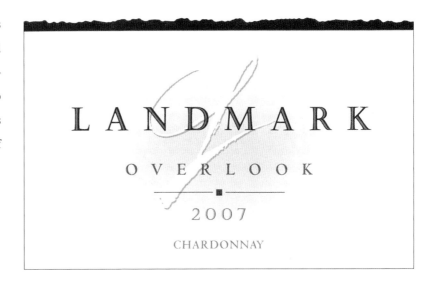

Wine & Fare

Overlook Chardonnay
(100% chardonnay)

Pair with seafood, shellfish, roast chicken and pork roast with fruit, as well as pastas with cream sauces.

Grand Detour Pinot Noir
(100% pinot noir)

Pair with game, duck and salmon, in addition to mushroom-accented dishes.

Steel Plow Syrah
(100% syrah)

Pair with a wide range of grilled and braised meats, as well as tomato-based dishes with savory herbs.

Tastings
Open to the public daily, year-round

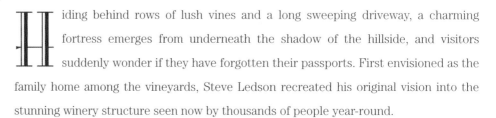

Ledson Winery & Vineyards

Kenwood

Hiding behind rows of lush vines and a long sweeping driveway, a charming fortress emerges from underneath the shadow of the hillside, and visitors suddenly wonder if they have forgotten their passports. First envisioned as the family home among the vineyards, Steve Ledson recreated his original vision into the stunning winery structure seen now by thousands of people year-round.

Although the Ledson family has been farming in the area since 1862, Steve's 16,000-square-foot masterpiece, The Castle, has only been open to the public since 1999. As an eager young man, Steve gained success as a builder and developer with the advancement of his company Ledson Construction, but ached to replant his family's roots in the wine-growing business. With a knack for aesthetics, Steve transformed his land into a replicated French château in the heart of California's divine and inspirational wine country.

The Castle—as it is known to family, friends, locals and visitors alike—is a staple to any wine-tasting tour because of its enchanting allure. Located along Highway 12, just about an hour's drive from San Francisco, even barely out-of-towners flock to this majestic architectural gem with its brick façade and handcrafted woodwork. While most people are first curious just to see the gorgeous Old World-style castle up close, once inside they linger because of the taste of Ledson's palate-pleasing wines. Well-manicured lawns, a rose garden, a perfect picnic spot under the shade of giant oak trees, a welcoming foyer with a grand wooden staircase, a gourmet market, and elegant tasting rooms all invite you to join in the romance of the setting.

Top Left: A bottle of Ledson Winery's flagship varietal merlot still continues to be a favorite.
Photograph by Elke Wolff

Bottom Left: Owner and winemaker Steve Ledson pauses in the picnic area of The Castle.
Photograph by Elke Wolff

Facing Page: From the front of The Castle, the view looks out over the main fountain, the vineyards and surrounding hills.
Photograph by M.J. Wickham

Ledson Winery introduced its first public vintage in 1997 prior to the finished construction of The Castle, and after rave reviews for the merlot, continued to surprise with other top-notch wines, including sauvignon blanc, chardonnay, pinot noir, barbera, sangiovese, zinfandel, syrah, petite sirah, cabernet sauvignon and more. Celebrating its 10-year anniversary in 2009, Ledson Winery basks in the glow of the California sun and soaks up plenty of commercial success with over 70 award-winning varieties like the sauvignon blanc earning the sweepstakes at the Sonoma County Harvest Fair and the Russian River Zinfandel, Amy's Vineyard receiving a 4-Star Gold Medal at the prestigious Orange County Fair, among many others; the Ledsons take care to meticulously farm the vineyards and take pride in sourcing the best grapes.

Besides establishing a Sonoma County landmark reminiscent of the residences of European royalty, Steve has used his life-long ambition and compassion to take on many other endeavors. With the continued fortune of Ledson's popular Wine Club, now with nine separate variations and thousands of devoted members, Steve took his passion for family, friends and determination on the road.

Right: Once inside the doors of the main hall, the grand staircase is reminiscent of classic, elegant decor.
Photograph courtesy of Ledson Winery & Vineyards

Facing Page Top: Winding up the driveway from Highway 12, The Castle welcomes visitors from around the world.
Photograph by Robert Holmes

Facing Page Bottom Left: Guests swirl and sip while mingling in one of the winery's nine tasting rooms.
Photograph by Forrest Galt

Facing Page Bottom Right: The gourmet marketplace is a wonderful last stop for visitors to picnic outside or purchase wine and other treats to go.
Photograph by M.J. Wickham

By bringing the luxury of a winery to the heart of a city in order to provide a more social atmosphere, Steve took on the quaint town plaza of Sonoma and opened the Ledson Hotel and Harmony Lounge. Perfect for a weekend away or just an indulgent place to sip and enjoy light plates while people-watching in the bustling square, the hotel and lounge have enjoyed acclaim both locally and nationwide. With six royal suites, the Ledson Hotel and Harmony Lounge caters to visitors' every need. The hospitality staff greets guests with a bottle of wine and can even set up complimentary VIP tastings or a picnic lunch at one or both of Ledson's affiliated wineries.

Steve is as dedicated to his community as he is to growing good grapes, and the service he provides to local kids does not go unnoticed or unappreciated. By establishing the Harmony Foundation for Children, which provides support and learning opportunities to underprivileged children in need, the Ledson family, Jeff Bridges, Dwight Clark and Michael McDonald have been integral in promoting this worthy cause. The Harmony Foundation has been able to give hundreds of thousands of dollars in grants to schools, children's programs and special cases all benefiting today's youth. Steve and the Ledson family's desire to give back to the community is due in part to their unique brand of generous hospitality and the fact that true character does not grow on vines.

Top Left: Ledson Hotel and Harmony Lounge is prominently located on the Historic Sonoma Plaza.
Photograph by Forrest Galt

Middle Left: In one of six royal rooms, guests can order an after-dinner drink or enjoy the view of the square from the balcony.
Photograph by Robert Holmes

Bottom Left: Hotel guests and locals indulge in beverages and small plates beneath the hotel in the Harmony Lounge.
Photograph by Forrest Galt

Facing Page: The trophy room encases distinct bottles with its award ribbons and doubles as a private-tasting cove for preferred Wine Club members.
Photograph by M.J. Wickham

Even though The Castle at Ledson Winery may take you back in time and urge you to look for a glass slipper, the setting is still humble Sonoma County with its tall grasses, fresh air and the satisfied hint of sophistication that only wine country can leave with you. The Castle's charm is hard to resist; visitors flock to Ledson Winery year-round to taste some of its magical wines and linger in the tranquil scenery. With many distinctive honors, the variety of Ledson wines helps to make every guest happy no matter what their taste buds crave. Visitors never fail to appreciate the meticulous design and thoughtful development of Steve's many endeavors. The impeccable hospitality and exquisite atmosphere, along with the unparalleled taste of each extraordinary wine, are what keep people coming back.

WINE & FARE

Russian River "Baldocci" Zinfandel
Pair with smoked duck breast on crostini.

Russian River Pinot Noir
Pair with roast pear and celery soup and bruschetta with garlic and basil.

Sonoma Valley Legend
Pair with Oysters Rockefeller.

Alexander Valley Cabernet Franc
Pair with Mocha Pot de Crème.

Tastings
Open to the public daily, year-round

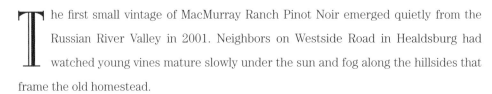

MacMurray Ranch

Healdsburg

The first small vintage of MacMurray Ranch Pinot Noir emerged quietly from the Russian River Valley in 2001. Neighbors on Westside Road in Healdsburg had watched young vines mature slowly under the sun and fog along the hillsides that frame the old homestead.

Less than 10 vintages later MacMurray Ranch Pinot Noir is a critic's choice, on allocation from coast to coast.

"We had a 150-year head start," says Kate MacMurray, whose family name adorns the label. "This land has been farmed since the 1850s, and whatever grows here seems to absorb a little of the magic of the ranch."

Kate's father, the late actor Fred MacMurray, bought the homestead and ranch in 1941 from the pioneer family who had been among the first settlers along the Middle Reach of the Russian River. After his death in 1991, Kate's family decided that the best way to keep the 1,500 acres open and in agriculture was to turn to wine grapes, which had replaced plum trees and hops vines all along the river.

The maturing of the first vines, planted in 1996, coincided with the arrival of a young winemaker from Tasmania, Susan Doyle, degreed in viticulture and enology, and who had made pinot noir in Australia and Burgundy and for a couple of California wineries. Susan also had very clear ideas about pinot noir.

Top Left: MacMurray Ranch is private but open for select community events.
Photograph by Joel Ottersbach

Bottom Left: Winemaker Susan Doyle (left) and Kate MacMurray (right) stop at the entrance to the barn.
Photograph by Brad Mollath

Facing Page: A crisp winter view from the high country of MacMurray Ranch reveals a backdrop of proud Pacific redwoods.
Photograph by Joel Ottersbach

Above Top: Kate and her dog Frankie relax in the MacMurray Ranch homestead surrounded by the estate vineyards.
Photograph by M.J. Wickham

Above Middle: The rustic and elegant MacMurray dining room has seen many home-cooked family meals.
Photograph by M.J. Wickham

Above Bottom: With more than 150 years of farming history, MacMurray Ranch honors its past as future vintages ripen in the vineyards.
Photograph by M.J. Wickham

Left: MacMurray Ranch is nestled in the heart of the Russian River Valley, a region celebrated for its world-class pinot noir and pinot gris wines.
Photograph by Joel Ottersbach

"At first, I focused on the estate vineyards," Susan recalls, "trying out clone and rootstock combinations, trellising regimes, low-impact farming practices. Little changes make a big difference with pinot noir."

Susan uses her well-honed intuition as well as her training in making the MacMurray wines: If you spend enough time in the vineyards, you get a sense of what's going on there, an awareness that comes from someplace other than the intellect. Susan famously delayed harvesting one of her top blocks when every material indicator said to go ahead. All the numbers were right, but she had a sense that something special was happening there. The result? Top scores from the judges and rave reviews from the critics.

As her Russian River Pinot Noir gained acclaim, Susan ranged farther afield, looking for the best grapes from the best places: the nearby Sonoma Coast, the Santa Lucia Highlands of Monterey County, the distant Santa Rita Hills of the Central Coast.

Right: The autumn vineyards of MacMurray Ranch display an array of fiery colors as harvest ends.
Photograph by M.J. Wickham

Facing Page Top: The MacMurray Ranch homestead sits under a majestic oak that shades it from the morning sun.
Photograph by Joel Ottersbach

Facing Page Bottom Left: In front of the homestead, lawn, gardens, vineyards and hills create a special sense of place.
Photograph by M.J. Wickham

Facing Page Bottom Right: The Russian River meanders through MacMurray Ranch on its way to the Pacific Ocean.
Photograph by M.J. Wickham

Susan helped design custom-crush facilities at the Gallo winery in nearby Healdsburg, equipped to accommodate the delicate pinot noir grapes. To expand the possibilities for her wines, she downsized even farther, with a "micro-winery" equipped with a little basket press and fermenters barely larger than hot tubs. "You really have to stay in touch with pinot noir as it develops," Susan explains, "and working small makes it all a bit easier. It's rather intimate, actually, like staying up with a fretting child."

Kate MacMurray agrees with Susan's approach. "Every wine, every vintage," she says, "is like a new child in the family. I am often asked which of the wines is my favorite, the pinot noir, the pinot gris, this one or that one. How can you choose?"

Kate enjoys walking the estate vineyards with Susan during the growing season. "I learn something in every conversation," she says. "Susan talks about the soil and the sun, and I take that with me when I travel and present the wines. We have very different vocabularies about wine, but we share a single point of view. I know little places around the property by their old names, and Susan knows them by the vines. She'll say they are getting great results on the first and second blocks in the Upper Valley, and I'll think that she's talking about the Pioneer Tree or Spring House Hill or Sleeping Lady."

Above: Fog moves up the Russian River Valley like clockwork, cloaking the vineyards and coaxing flavor and character into the pinot noir vines as it cools them.
Photograph by Joel Ottersbach

Facing Page: The flavors of autumn grace a table on the porch of the homestead, a perfect complement to MacMurray Ranch pinot noir and pinot gris wines.
Photograph by M.J. Wickham

History is a tangible part of MacMurray Ranch, as real and as present as the hills, the homestead and the creeks. Kate loves the way the light moves over the vineyards and how the wind shifts each summer afternoon and cool air sweeps across the rows of pinot gris and through the old house. That's the time to be on the porch with a glass of wine.

Kate has these enduring sense memories from her childhood on the ranch, and she gets the same sensations when she tastes the wines—a scent of the blackberries by the creek, the cherries from the orchard, the herbs in the kitchen garden. It all feels right and true.

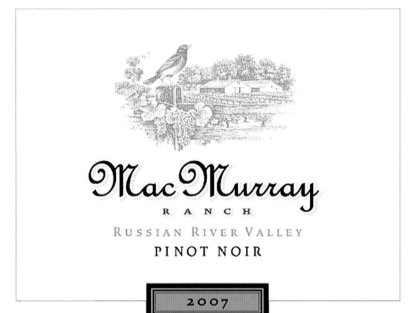

WINE & FARE

MacMurray Ranch Russian River Valley Pinot Noir
*Pair with bay-rubbed rib-eye steak with wild mushrooms
and pinot noir reduction.*

MacMurray Ranch Sonoma Coast Pinot Gris
*Pair with smoked trout on a salad of butter lettuce with sliced
Gravenstein apples and candied walnuts.*

Tastings
Not open to the public

Matanzas Creek Winery

Santa Rosa

Matanzas Creek Winery was founded in 1977, a time when few California wineries were focused on creating handcrafted, premium-quality wine. Since its first vintage, the winery has been inspired by the promise of producing world-class wines that showcase the special qualities and diversity of Sonoma County.

Located in the northwest corner of the Sonoma Valley, Matanzas Creek's home in Bennett Valley existed for many years in quiet obscurity—bountifully sustaining an agricultural community that had all but forgotten the valley's pre-Prohibition viticultural roots. The founding of Matanzas Creek on the site of a retired dairy farm would bring worldwide attention to this quiet, bucolic community.

From humble beginnings, Matanzas Creek was quickly catapulted into the national spotlight when its 1979 vintage of chardonnay won critical acclaim throughout the United States. During that vintage, the wine went through an unintended, secondary malolactic fermentation—a technique that was uncommon at the time. The resulting wine was slightly buttery, yet fruit forward, and would become a major influence on the style of chardonnay that California made famous. In turn, Matanzas Creek would become an indelible name in the industry.

Top Left: In the 1990s Matanzas Creek planted one acre of lavender to augment the beautiful estate gardens.
Photograph by M.J. Wickham

Bottom Left: The deck off the tasting room has amazing views of the estate below.
Photograph by M.J. Wickham

Facing Page: The 120-acre Jackson Park vineyard has established Matanzas Creek's leadership role in the Bennett Valley winegrowing community.
Photograph by M.J. Wickham

Top: Matanzas Creek is also known for its estate gardens, which include native grasses, olive trees and exotic perennials.
Photograph by M.J. Wickham

Bottom: Two species of lavender are grown at Matanzas Creek: Provence and Grosso. Provence is grown for culinary use and Grosso for bath and home products.
Photograph by M.J. Wickham

Top: The 4,500 lavender plants are in full bloom by early summer, making Matanzas Creek a renowned travel destination.
Photograph by M.J. Wickham

Bottom: Matanzas Creek recently added a bocce ball court in its gardens, which visitors are encouraged to enjoy.
Photograph by M.J. Wickham

Besides its chardonnay, Matanzas Creek is known for sauvignon blanc and cool climate wines including merlot, pinot noir and syrah, all of which are grown around the winery's Bennett Valley home. In 2003 Bennett Valley was carved out of the Sonoma Valley appellation and was recognized as Sonoma County's 13th American Viticultural Area, formally acknowledging the special climate, soil profile, topography and aspects of the area. Bennett Valley is defined by three mountains—Sonoma, Bennett and Taylor—that capture the marine influences of the nearby Pacific Ocean—an effect called the Petaluma Wind Gap—causing the temperature profile to be similar to the Russian River Valley. This cooling effect represents the vanguard of modern viticulture: to plant grapes at extreme locations and take the slow path to ripeness.

In addition to wine, Matanzas Creek is known for its estate gardens, which are an eclectic blend of wind-blown native grasses; delicate, billowing olive trees; exotic perennials and its famed lavender.

Above: The Matanzas Creek tasting room is open to the public year-round.
Photograph by M.J. Wickham

Facing Page: The wine press is, of course, an integral component at Matanzas Creek Winery.
Photograph by Katee Pendergast-McGee

MATANZAS CREEK WINERY

The lavender fields were planted in the early '90s, consisting of a one-acre plot with over 4,500 plants. As with grapes, lavender is well suited to the estate's climate and well-drained soils. Harvested in early summer, the lavender is hand-cut for use in culinary, bath, body and home products, which are available only in the Matanzas Creek tasting room or online.

Celebrated wines, gorgeous gardens and a warm and friendly sense of hospitality continue to make Matanzas Creek a sought-after wine-country destination more then 30 years after its founding.

WINE & FARE

Matanzas Creek Chardonnay
Pair with penne with feta and hazelnut pesto.

Matanzas Creek Sauvignon Blanc
Pair with key lime pie.

Matanzas Creek Merlot
Pair with marinated rack of lamb with roasted potatoes.

Matanzas Creek Pinot Noir
Pair with glazed duck with pistachios.

Tastings
Open to the public daily, year-round

Matrix Winery

Healdsburg

Matrix is an artisan winery in the making. Planting new vines on this undulating property gives Ken and Diane Wilson a chance to move into the Russian River Valley and to produce pinot noirs. The Wilsons are dedicated to producing premium wines and pride themselves on finding just the right land to farm and to plant, with just the right grapes for Diane to make her award-winning wines. At Matrix, the dream is to make Russian River pinot noirs and Bordeaux varietals from this beautiful west Dry Creek vineyard.

At Matrix, the labor-intensive farming practices produce low-yielding vineyards, resulting in grapes with an astounding concentration of flavors. Diane's hands-on approach and intimate attention to detail will bring the flavors to the forefront with this collection of wines, powerful yet elegant. Set in a curving, hilly section of the Russian River Valley, the vineyard undulates over the hilltops creating a beautiful abstract of vines. Ken Wilson has an eye for land, and he plants his vineyards as if they were a painter's canvas. His vineyards are always a joy to see as they conform to the land like the perfect pair of jeans. The payoff is clearly in the glass. Newly opened and waiting for its winery renovation, Matrix has already garnered many gold medals and media acclaim. Those who have already discovered this elegant wine can enjoy the cozy Matrix tasting room, walk the gardens that adorn the grounds or venture onto the deck to enjoy panoramic views of the coastal mountains and sweeping vineyard vistas.

Top & Middle Left: The Russian River Valley is an incredible backdrop for sipping fine wines, from chardonnay to cabernet.
Photographs by M.J. Wickham

Bottom Left & Facing Page: The finest vineyards and a gifted winemaker are the keys to Matrix's acclaim.
Photographs by M.J. Wickham

Mazzocco Sonoma Winery

Healdsburg

The Dry Creek Valley stretches an arm eastward toward Alexander Valley, creating a natural saddle in the beautiful Sonoma County landscape. It is on this crest we find Mazzocco sitting comfortably on the backs of these two legendary wine valleys. This family-owned artisan winery has the spirit of wild horses—a spirit running free from their mountainside vineyards into the barrels. The result: The wines of Mazzocco are a thunderous collection, rich and captivating. Noted for its zinfandels and classic Bordeaux varietals, the winery practices a vineyard-driven approach to winemaking. The winery's history and tradition combined with a reputation for innovation have made it one of the most distinctive and sought-after brands in California.

The label may say Dry Creek Valley, but Ken and Diane Wilson have vineyards that are situated at elevations reaching up to 2,400 feet with views of the Pacific Ocean on hillsides seemingly suited only to a mountain goat. These remote sites are ideal for low-yielding vineyards that produce astounding concentrations of flavor. The Mazzocco approach is hands on, embracing all aspects of the vines' health and physiological development. It derives from years of experience cultivating in this unique regional terroir. All vineyard work and winemaking techniques are done by hand and aimed at bringing out the unique, intrinsic character and true spirit of each individual varietal. The resulting wines stimulate the senses, warm the heart and evoke a feeling of well being.

Top Left: Mazzocco welcomes guests from all over the world for tours and tastings.
Photograph by M.J. Wickham

Bottom Left & Facing Page: The winery's signature vineyard-designate zinfandels are robust and sumptuous yet individual in nature.
Photographs by M.J. Wickham

French-born winemaker Antoine Favero believes that wines should be nurtured rather than produced. This nurturing originates in the vineyards by listening to the vines and providing for them a balanced environment to develop maximum color, fleshy tannins and engaging aromas. Antoine accomplishes this by matching the vines to the perfect soil, climate and exposure. He specializes in wines that express the unique varietal and terroir characteristics of each vineyard site. Bordeaux varietals are his passion, he says, and zinfandels his obsession. "I'm constantly aiming for a velvety mouth entry in my wines—a trait that has become my signature."

Left: The tasting room lounge is a great place to relax, sip wine and enjoy the breathtaking views.
Photographs by M.J. Wickham

Facing Page: Mazzocco's award-winning wines are culled from fertile mountain vineyards.
Photograph by M.J. Wickham

Mazzocco Winery dedicates itself to crafting luscious wines that are powerful yet elegant, long-lasting in the palate and long-lived in the cellar. A visit to the winery offers an exceptional opportunity to experience the passion behind the wine. Tasting in the stylish tasting room or relaxing by the fountain in comfy lounge furniture with a glass of highly acclaimed wine offers the chance to drink in the splendor of Dry Creek Valley. Scheduled live music and wine and food pairings by acclaimed local chefs can also be enjoyed at the winery. The Mazzocco tasting experience is unparalleled in wine country.

MAZZOCCO
SONOMA

2006 DRY CREEK VALLEY
ZINFANDEL
HEALDSBURG · CALIFORNIA
WARM SPRINGS RANCH

PROPRIETORS: KEN & DIANE WILSON • WINEMAKER: ANTOINE FAVERO

WINE & FARE

Mazzocco Cabernet Sauvignon
Pair with braised lamb shank with vegetables and fava beans.

Mazzocco Stuhlmuller Reserve Chardonnay
Pair with hazelnut chicken in a prosciutto cream sauce and fresh greens.

Mazzocco Petit Sirah Pony Reserve
Pair with a sliced steak sandwich with gorgonzola butter and caramelized onions.

Mazzocco Warm Springs Ranch Zinfandel
Pair with an apple and turkey sausage and wild-mushroom lasagna.

Tastings
Open to the public daily, year-round

Michel-Schlumberger
Wine Estate

Healdsburg

Set in a countryside where only Steinbeck's words can do justice, the vineyards of Michel-Schlumberger sit on a stretch of 100 benchland and mountaintop acres. The Spanish Mission-style estate adds distinct character to the winery and leaves visitors with an impressive architectural image. Rightly named Wine Creek Canyon, the region lies in a pocket of the western Dry Creek Valley hillsides, just 17 miles off the Pacific Coast. The creek flows through wild ravines of commanding redwoods and courses through rolling upland and benchland vineyards before ending its journey to the valley floor. Cool growing temperatures on south-sloping terraces let the fruit ripen evenly, naturally. The consistent exposure and well-drained soils yield perfect grapes. All 100 acres are organically farmed with a portion of the property being a certified wildlife preserve. Here, the land is everything; it defines the character of wine.

The winery's story begins in 1977. It was then that Jean-Jacques Michel discovered ideal soils among California's Sonoma County wine country for the Old World style of wines he desired to produce. Within two years he had established Domaine Michel Wine Estate—a quality-oriented, limited-bottling operation with strong potential. Jacques Schlumberger joined Jean-Jacques as a business partner in 1991. As time continued, Jacques saw opportunities for growth and led the establishment in a new direction, yet still held strong the founding virtues. In 1993 he took majority ownership and renamed the winery Michel-Schlumberger Wine Estate. He remodeled the company for today's

Top Left: Officially founded in 1979, the estate welcomes visitors from around the world.
Photograph by M.J. Wickham

Bottom Left: The winemakers believe in blending varieties for complexity; their reds harness the ripe, raw power of the new world with the elegant reins of the old.
Photograph by M.J. Wickham

Facing Page: The Spanish Mission-style estate glows at night.
Photograph by M.J. Wickham

market, bringing in state-of-the-art machinery, and planted a wider variety of healthy new vines. And he was the perfect person to do so—boasting more than 400 years of vintner lineage from Alsace. Jacques also adds a musical touch to the winery's character, with a strong appreciation for classical instruments. The summer brings a weekly musical series to the courtyard: a perfect accompaniment to Michel-Schlumberger wine.

In 1993 winemaker Fred Payne hired Michael Brunson as cellar worker. Mike worked his way through the ranks and became assistant winemaker in the late '90s. In 2005 he took over the reins as winemaker from his mentor. Mike, like Jacques, had his mind set on high-quality, small-lot yields to capture the best flavor. With a countryside so full of life and personality, Mike knew wine drinkers would love the product. And it's a countryside he knows well, having spent five years in the fields helping

Fred to replant phylloxera-ridden vines that had taken over. Nursing the land back to health, Fred and Mike used modern clones, low-vigor rootstock, dense spacing and new trellising to achieve the vitality they and Jacques had planned. Mike knows how to capture the varied terroir better than anyone.

Above Left: The tasting salon is just one of many places where wine can be sampled on the property.
Photograph by M.J. Wickham

Above Right: The reflecting pool serves as the serene courtyard's focal point.
Photograph by M.J. Wickham

Facing Page: Equal parts picturesque and educational, the winery's popular "Green Tour" of the organic vineyards culminates with a memorable hillside tasting.
Photograph by M.J. Wickham

Michel-Schlumberger encapsulates the most appealing aspects of the land and the people who tend to it. With 14 varietals in all, wine lovers can find a bottle to suit any meal—La Brume Chardonnay, Pinot Blanc or Cabernet Sauvignon match the dynamic cuisine of California. In addition to traditional samplings, Michel-Schlumberger offers artisan cheese tastings, vertical tastings, vineyard tours and hillside tastings—enough to draw visitors from across the country.

WINE & FARE

Coteaux Sauvages Estate Red

Pair with wild mushroom soup or steaks in green peppercorn sauce.

La Brume Chardonnay

Marked by a hint of orange blossom, ginger and pear, this wine pairs well with Nantucket seafood salad or Asian chicken thighs with curry and lime.

Deux Terres Bordeaux Blend

Pair with rich red pepper soup, honey grilled lamb chops or a juniper berry pork roast.

Tastings
Open to the public daily, year-round

Papapietro Perry Winery

Healdsburg

I f you like pinot noir, Sonoma County is the place to be. The down-home, casual local color certainly makes the area appealing as well. Here two families came together with a shared love of pinot noir and food. Ben Papapietro and Bruce Perry both understood that pinot noir is an approachable variety, the best with food, and doesn't need to age as long as other red varietals. Longtime friends, the two united with one mission: to promote the union of good food, good wine and good friends.

The Papapietro Perry Winery cellar sits in the heart of Dry Creek Valley, but it wasn't always there. In 1980 Ben began producing garagista wines as a hobby—produced in a garage, a sort of do-it-yourself operation. Bruce soon joined in Ben's quest for the perfect wine. The two secured enough grapes to make five gallons of pinot, liked what they had, and so the deal was sealed. By 1990 the two had found consistent sources for their grapes, and set about perfecting their craft. In 1998 Papapietro Perry was born with their first release of only 75 cases.

Papapietro Perry Winery acquires all of its grapes from the Russian River, Anderson and Dry Creek Valleys. These are perfect vineyards for Papapietro Perry's wines, and when the grapes come in, Ben, Bruce and crew—along with a few fun-loving friends and family—only handle the fruit by hand. Consistency is imperative, and so the winemakers insist on making evenness part of their style. To truly let the grapes speak for themselves, all other elements need to be carefully managed. The team cold-soaks its grapes before fermenting and always uses the same kind of cultured yeast and French oak François Frères barrels. Because of this determination to cultivate the best wines under the best variables, Papapietro Perry Winery garnered critical acclaim very quickly upon opening.

Top Left: The Papapietro Perry zinfandel and pinot noir express the character of their parent vineyards.
Photograph by Kelly McManus

Bottom Left: An old basket press nods to Papapietro's beginnings—some old equipment, a garage and wine-loving friends.
Photograph by M.J. Wickham

Facing Page: The tasting room boasts stunning views of Timbercrest Farms.
Photograph by M.J. Wickham

Papapietro Perry Winery specializes in small lots of handcrafted pinot noir and zinfandel produced from the finest grapes. Bruce and Ben work closely with growers and carefully select vineyards whose fruit exemplifies the most delicious and complex flavors the region has to offer. Using a non-interventionist style of winemaking, Ben allows the fruit to shine through in each bottle he produces.

A great opportunity to sample the fruit of these Sonoma County vineyards is to try one of Papapietro Perry Winery's single-vineyard designate wines—a true taste of a given spot in a given time.

Papapietro Perry Winery produces multiple pinot noirs, including vineyard blends, single-vineyard designates and clonal designates as well as several remarkable zinfandels.

Top Left: The passion of winery owners Bruce and Renae Perry and Yolanda and Ben Papapietro is evident in every bottle.
Photograph by M.J. Wickham

Middle Left: Guests enjoy sampling Papapietro Perry's handcrafted wines in the tasting room.
Photograph by M.J. Wickham

Bottom Left: Winery dog Ruby Perry enjoys fetching tennis balls on her daily run in the vineyard.
Photograph by M.J. Wickham

Facing Page: The tasting room features bars handmade from barrel staves.
Photograph by M.J. Wickham

Master sommelier Madeline Triffon once called pinot noir "sex in a glass," and without question there is something spicy and seductive about Papapietro Perry's wines. Each wine is brilliantly complex, intriguingly vibrant and, as they like to say with a little twinkle in their eyes, "So good, you'll want to swallow."

PAPAPIETRO PERRY

WINE & FARE

Pinot Noir
Pair with salmon, ham, duck, mushrooms—almost anything!

Zinfandel
Pair with hearty pastas, pizza, sausage and steaks.

Tastings
Open to the public daily, year-round

Passalacqua Winery

Healdsburg

Passalacqua Winery's Dry Creek Valley home marks the confluence of dramatic natural beauty, varied terroir and treasured family traditions of winemaking and winegrowing. From a knoll with beautiful views of this rustic, rural appellation, Jason and Noelle Passalacqua continue their family's storied Sonoma County history with a new generation of wines pairing the region's pioneering past and modern sophistication.

The Passalacqua tradition began with Jason's great-grandfather Francesco, who came to California from Italy in the late 1800s. Francesco eventually founded Fitch Mountain Winery, one of the first in Healdsburg. Years after Francesco's passing and the loss of the winery in a fire, his wife Rachel purchased another winery up the road and willed it to her daughter Edith, whose historic label appears on today's Passalacqua wines. Blended with this winemaking history is that of Noelle's family, brought from France to the Santa Clara Valley by her great-grandfather Jean Oscamou. From a homestead vineyard, Jean produced and shared his wine with the Jesuits at Santa Clara University, later to become Jason and Noelle's alma mater. Their Italian and French heritages now dovetail into the uniquely family-focused production of elegant California wines.

Top Left: Jason and Noelle Passalacqua pause with their son, Luca, and daughter, Mariella, in the gardens at Passalacqua Winery.
Photograph by M.J. Wickham

Bottom Left: Passalacqua chardonnay paired with cheese and fruit waits to be enjoyed with a garden view.
Photograph by M.J. Wickham

Facing Page: Passalacqua Winery's spectacular setting on a knoll overlooks Dry Creek Valley. Visitors enjoy sweeping views from the redwood-shaded veranda.
Photograph by M.J. Wickham

Above Top: Passalacqua produces small lots of food-friendly wines to enjoy with family and friends.
Photograph by Charlie Gesell

Above Middle: A signature welcome to the Passalacqua tasting room and gardens.
Photograph by M.J. Wickham

Above Bottom: Passalacqua wines are sold exclusively through the winery's Dry Creek Valley tasting room.
Photograph by M.J. Wickham

Left: Fountains in the lower garden lend the perfect background notes to this exquisite setting.
Photograph by M.J. Wickham

No matter their level of expertise, drinkers of Passalacqua wine experience a comfortable, approachable taste of the valley's bounty resulting from careful coaxing of the fruit's best qualities. Passalacqua produces about 5,000 cases a year, for purchase exclusively through its tasting room, selling out of every varietal among the coveted, food-friendly wines. Award-winning winemaker Margaret Davenport directs the small-lot production with a focused, handcrafted approach yielding the perfect equilibrium in the glass. Transferring her extensive knowledge and experience from producing millions of cases per year, she enjoys being hands-on from vineyard to bottle, crafting each wine according to a personal philosophy of pure varietal intensity tempered with balance and finesse.

Wines bearing the Passalacqua name are also a testament to the vineyards from which they come, where small blocks of select fruit capture the essence of Sonoma County. Grapes are sourced from the finest plots around, including that of Jason's parents Tom and Sandi, who grow cabernet on the southern boundary of Dry Creek Valley. In fact, cabernets from this diverse and ruggedly beautiful vineyard have become so highly regarded that the winery's block-select vintages are only procured through exclusive offerings.

Above: Vintage barrels line the wisteria-shaded entry.
Photograph by M.J. Wickham

Facing Page: Passalacqua cabernets from the T.R. Passalacqua Vineyard are prized for their pure varietal intensity and finesse.
Photograph by M.J. Wickham

Though the winery is well known for cabernets and zinfandels, every varietal offered by the Passalacquas speaks to their heritage; Radici della Famiglia, for example, joins French and Italian varietals in a Tuscan-style blend named for treasured family roots. Visitors—especially those who opt to take a tour or book a private tasting—will experience the winery's beautiful, bucolic setting of meandering gardens, towering redwoods and spectacular views and enjoy not only a respite in the setting where Jason and Noelle have made their home, but a unique taste of winemaking and winegrowing tradition as well.

WINE & FARE

Dry Creek Valley Barrel Fermented Chardonnay

Pair with butternut squash ravioli with brown butter-sage sauce. Jason Passalacqua makes the ravioli by hand, just as his Noni Dee taught him.

Dry Creek Valley Maple Vineyard Zinfandel

Pair with roasted duck breast with cherry sauce. The hints of fruit and spice in this zinfandel bring out the best flavors of the recipe.

Radici della Famiglia—Tuscan Blend

Pair with pollo e funghi selvaggi con il polenta (chicken with wild mushrooms and polenta). For many local Italian families, it is a tradition to gather your own mushrooms in the fall, making this dish even more enjoyable. Jason was raised with this tradition and has already begun passing it on to his own two children, Mariella and Luca.

Dry Creek Valley Cabernet Sauvignon

Pair with rustic short rib ragout with fresh pasta. The grapes from T.R. Passalacqua Ranch give this cabernet blackberry and plum flavors, and two years in French oak add smoke and spice that, together, perfectly complement this savory dish.

Tastings
Open to the public

Pellegrini Family Vineyards

Santa Rosa

So much of winemaking is allowing the vineyard to speak: How does one enable wines to show their intrinsic personality? The basic elements of soil, climate and man's farming techniques encapsulate the definition of terroir, thereby assuring distinction in the grapes themselves. Allowing that fruit to be turned into wine through meticulous attention to detail by traditional artisan methods is the fundamental principle of producing wines of breed and character. The foundation of Pellegrini Family Vineyards is built upon this premise, relying on sustainable, organic farming methods and non-interventional winemaking that includes native yeast fermentations with minimal manipulation. The state-of-the-art winery was designed to handle the family's estate-grown grapes in a clean and gentle manner, with varied vat capacity ideally suited for small-lot handcrafted winemaking.

The story begins when the Pellegrini brothers, Nello and Gino, left Tuscany for America at the start of the 1900s. During the 1920s, they became grape merchants, shipping grapes from Sonoma County growers to the San Francisco produce terminal and by rail to the nation's eastern cities for home winemaking. Although the Volstead Act restricted the production of wine for sale, each household was permitted to make 200 gallons of wine each year for personal use—so there was a thriving business in grapes. After the repeal of Prohibition, the brothers founded the Pellegrini Wine Company in 1933. It was the reawakening of the California wine industry after a 13-year slumber; and soon the Pellegrini name became known locally for solid Sonoma County red table wine in many of San Francisco's restaurants and retail shops.

Top Left: Robert, Jean, Aida and Richard Pellegrini.
Photograph courtesy of The Pellegrini Family archive

Middle Left: Just before harvest, zinfandel grape clusters at the Pellegrini Eight Cousins Vineyard reach full potential.
Photograph by Susan Williams Pellegrini

Bottom Left: The open-top fermentation vats and barrels are used for handcrafted artisan winemaking.
Photograph by Susan Williams Pellegrini

Facing Page: The vista of Olivet Lane Vineyard and Pellegrini Winery reveals cloud-shrouded Mt. St. Helena in the distance.
Photograph by Susan Williams Pellegrini

By the '50s a new generation of Pellegrinis took the reins. Under Vincent Pellegrini, the company transitioned into wholesale wine distribution and importing, representing a broad selection of producers from California and Europe, establishing itself as one of the largest wine distributors in California at that time. Later, in 1973, Vincent and his wife Ida acquired 65 acres in Russian River Valley with the intention of going full circle and becoming winegrowers. Chardonnay and pinot noir vines were selected on the notion that those varieties would thrive in this relatively cool region frequently buffered by morning and evening fog from the coast. Olivet Lane Vineyard, named for the 150 or so old olive trees that line the entrance, today is considered one of the heritage vineyards for pinot noir and chardonnay in the region.

Following a 15-year hiatus from bottling wines, Robert Pellegrini, a member of the third generation, led the family back into winemaking in 1977. In the early '80s the first wines from Olivet Lane Vineyard were released, and 10 years later they were joined by wines from Cloverdale Ranch—a 47-acre vineyard in Alexander Valley planted to Bordeaux varieties. Most recently, members of the fourth generation contributed to the development of a nine-acre zinfandel vineyard in Russian River Valley. Grafted from cuttings taken from

Above Left: Bottles of Cloverdale Ranch Alexander Valley Cabernet Sauvignon and Merlot, Pellegrini Milestone, Pellegrini Zinfandel, and Olivet Lane Russian River Valley Chardonnay and Pinot Noir are the end result of a careful process.
Photograph by Susan Williams Pellegrini

Middle Left: Cloverdale Ranch in Alexander Valley shows its pastoral elegance.
Photograph by Robert Pellegrini

Bottom Left: Old-vine cabernet sauvignon is trained in a split canopy.
Photograph by Robert Pellegrini

Facing Page: The original Pellegrini winery opened in 1933, with Nello, Mary and Esther Pellegrini at work.
Photograph courtesy of The Pellegrini Family archive

neighboring vines planted in the early 1900s, this young vineyard has already produced noteworthy wines that exhibit depth, balance and complexity.

Pellegrini Family Vineyards lays claim on a long stretch of history; the release of Milestone in 2008, a blend comprised of five Bordeaux varieties, in fact, celebrates the 75 years the family has been active in the California wine industry. The Pellegrini family looks upon this wine as a tribute to those who have gone before.

PELLEGRINI

Milestone

2006

SONOMA COUNTY RED WINE

*A Reserve Cuvée of
Merlot 53%, Cabernet Sauvignon 28%,
Petite Verdot 9%, Cabernet Franc 5%,
and Malbec 5%*

75 YEARS   1933-2008

WINE & FARE

Pellegrini Zinfandel—Russian River Valley

*Pair with Ida Pellegrini's pollo alla
cacciatore—chicken hunter-style.*

*Olivet Lane Estate Pinot Noir—
Russian River Valley*

*Pair with Janet Pellegrini's arista di maiale con
patatine—roast pork with potatoes.*

Cloverdale Ranch Merlot—Alexander Valley

*Pair with Ida Pellegrini's osso buco with risotto
zafferano—veal shank with saffron rice.*

Tastings
Open to the public daily, year-round

Quivira Vineyards

Healdsburg

The search for gold has become a bit of an anomaly in our common era, yet the old hunt led to the discovery of wonderful parts of the world. After the Spanish conquest of the Aztec kingdom, the conquistadors looked north for a similarly gold-laden territory called Quivira. Though the literal gold was a myth, the location where Quivira Vineyards now sits is overburdened with agricultural bliss. The exploration, in the long run, proved more than fruitful.

The confluence of Wine and Dry creeks is an idyllic setting, and anyone could understand why the Quivira crew chose this site for trailblazing into the future of agriculture. The modern-day manifestation of ancient land stewardship drives Pete and Terri Kight, proprietors of Quivira, with a steadfast principle of going beyond the purpose. That purpose, of course, is to make remarkable wine. But Quivira was determined to turn a business into a way of life.

Since 2005 Quivira has been a Demeter-certified Biodynamic winery. Biodynamic farming, in essence, is not just about organic or sustainable agricultural practices. The farm, under Biodynamic principles, is treated like a living organism, a self-sustaining system entirely responsible for creating and maintaining its individual health and vitality without any external and unnatural additions. Recycling back into the earth everything that has come from it means that what is unique about a vineyard is enhanced and concentrated over time. The result is wine that truly embodies its place of origin.

Top Left: Proprietor Pete Kight and winemaker Steven Canter put in some legwork at the vineyard.
Photograph by M.J. Wickham

Bottom Left: In keeping with its holistic approach to farming, Quivira produces estate-grown olive oil, honey and preserves, including red wine-poached figs.
Photograph by M.J. Wickham

Facing Page: A 55kW solar-electric system has supplied 100 percent of Quivira's energy needs since 2005.
Photograph by M.J. Wickham

Above: The Kight family—Pete, Ali, Terri and Preston—push Quivira to embody place of origin by specializing in zinfandel, sauvignon blanc and Rhône varietals like grenache, syrah and mourvèdre. The well-known Fig Tree Vineyard Sauvignon Blanc was named for the majestic 130-year-old Black mission fig that stands among its vines.
Photographs by M.J. Wickham

Left: Goat Trek Vineyard is approximately 1,300 feet above sea level. Of all Quivira's estate vineyards it is the most susceptible to ocean influences, experiencing cool nights.
Photograph by M.J. Wickham

The keys to Biodynamic farming are health—in terms of the estate as a whole—and balance—the farm in relation to its surroundings. This is an opportunity to reexamine our ancestors' knowledge of the land; soil, water and air have a natural system of checks and balances. Quivira reflects this Old World farming by nurturing the environment, not forcing it. There is a definitive cycle in this process. Compost and cover crops are the only fertilizers used—no pesticides can be found anywhere in the environment. By composting the winery's entire residue, the minerals carry the ideal local flavor. Controlling vine vigor while nurturing the soil supports not only the grapes but also a diversity of agricultural products. As well, several beyond-the-vine mechanisms, including a herd of goats to control overgrowth, push farming standards.

The culmination of the deeply rooted principles of Biodynamic farming, however, is the wine. Such close attention to stewardship of the land and its creatures produces the best wines, and Quivira Vineyards employed Steven Canter as head winemaker to craft wines that are the best expression of Quivira's terroir. Known for its Dry Creek Valley Zinfandel,

Top Left: Zinfandel excels on the hillside sites of Quivira's main estate vineyard, Wine Creek Ranch.
Photograph by M.J. Wickham

Middle Left: Since 1998 Quivira has been actively engaged in restoring Wine Creek, the Coho salmon- and Steelhead trout-spawning stream that winds through the center of the estate.
Photograph by M.J. Wickham

Bottom Left: Quivira's Biodynamic and organic garden is designed to educate visitors on farming and viticultural practices, as well as supply local markets with fresh produce.
Photograph by M.J. Wickham

Facing Page: The garden includes 120 raised redwood beds, a Biodynamic prep tower, pond, greenhouse and chicken coop.
Photograph by M.J. Wickham

QUIVIRA

DRY CREEK VALLEY

2006

Zinfandel

WINE CREEK RANCH

Quivira focuses on small-lot vines to showcase the best of what Dry Creek Valley has to offer. With sauvignon blanc, grenache and Rhône varietals, Quivira takes its wine to new possibilities, for there is no better product than one derived from holistic, responsible development. From the Biodynamic methods employed in the farm life, to the solar panels that produce all needed electricity, to the restoration of the Steelhead trout and Coho salmon habitat, Quivira musters every mechanism possible to produce incredible wines through extraordinary winemaking processes.

WINE & FARE

Quivira Sauvignon Blanc, Fig Tree Vineyard

Pair with a plate of fresh oysters or a green salad topped with baked goat cheese.

Quivira Grenache, Wine Creek Ranch

Pair with roast duck or cassoulet served with herbed potatoes and roasted vegetables.

Quivira Zinfandel, Wine Creek Ranch

Pair with spicy pork ragout and rosemary polenta.

Tastings
Open to the public daily, year-round

Robledo Family Winery

Sonoma

When World War II broke out, many men were sent overseas to fight, creating a shortage of labor in America. The United States collaborated with Mexico to begin the Bracero Program in which Mexican men and women were invited to work as laborers in America. Labor camps were established throughout the country. In 1949 Robledos began to settle in Healdsburg, where they worked in the vineyards. They built their reputation as master grafters in the wine industry, grafting thousands of acres in Napa and Sonoma counties, working on landscapes the same as their pueblo in Mexico.

Reynaldo Robledo was born in the pueblo Ataches, high atop the Sierra Madre Mountains in the state of Michoacan. In 1968 he left the Atacheo pueblo for California, finding migrant vineyard work at the Christian Brothers labor camp in the hot spot of the American grape economy. There, his father taught him about the vineyards. Very soon he realized the remarkable potential that could be found in well-developed winemaking, and he developed a passion that simply would not subside. Under his leadership he came to develop and farm hundreds of vineyard acres in Napa and Sonoma, finally culminating in the development of Robledo Family Winery.

Top Left: Reynaldo Robledo Sr. started it all.
Photograph by M.J. Wickham

Bottom Left: Maria's famous chicken enchiladas go perfectly at a tasting.
Photograph by M.J. Wickham

Facing Page: Robledo Family Winery embodies an Old World feel.
Photograph by M.J. Wickham

It was not until the mid-1980s that Reynaldo and his wife, Maria, decided to invest in some of their own property. They chose a piece of land—13 acres nestled in the cool appellation of Los Carneros, Napa—that was known as Rancho Rincon de Los Carneros when California was still part of Mexico. To honor this history, the couple kept the name for the ranch. From this spread of land, the Robledo family began to cultivate the fruit that would put Robledo Family Winery on the map. And it was here that Reynaldo brought his family into the business, teaching his young children how to prune, tie, sucker, lift wire, leaf the vines and do everything else that is involved in growing and harvesting.

Top Right: The tasting room is a great place to start.
Photograph by M.J. Wickham

Bottom Right: The Napa Carneros pinot noir at Rancho Rincon gets to the root of things.
Photograph by M.J. Wickham

Facing Page: At Rancho Maria in Sonoma Carneros, the vineyards are producing.
Photograph by M.J. Wickham

Now, Robledo Family Winery operates some 300 acres of vineyards across Sonoma, Napa and Lake County regions. Though most of the fruit harvested is sold to other wineries, Robledo Family Winery produces several varietals for its own fine wines, including a moscato. While the winery not only produces critically acclaimed wines—the 2006 sauvignon blanc was the gold medal winner at the 2008 *San Francisco Chronicle* wine competition and the 2008 Pacific Coast Oyster Competition, the 2006 pinot blanc gold medal winner at the 2008 Orange County Fair, Tempranillo gold medal winner at the 2008 California State Fair and the 2005 merlot won gold at the Florida State Fair—some notoriety has come from other sources: Robledo's 2006 chardonnay was served at the White House on Cinco de Mayo, and the winery has the distinction of being one of the first owned by a Mexican migrant vineyard worker.

To the family, each bottle of Robledo wine is a small triumph. Headed by a man seeking a better life, the organization practices old-school methods of showing rather than telling. As the next generation stepped into place, the winemakers learned skills in grape culture from the source. Everardo Robledo stood next to his father in the fields since childhood, watching the elder nurture the kind of fruit that has brought California to the wine industry forefront. For experience, there is no substitute for life-long exposure to the product. Winemaking, therefore, has become instinct for the Robledos.

Above: Robledo Family Winery is certainly multigenerational: Francisco, Vanessa, Everardo and Jenaro are standing and Emiliano, Maria, Reynaldo Sr. and Luis are sitting.
Photograph by M.J. Wickham

Facing Page: Robledo Family Winery features great picnic grounds.
Photograph by M.J. Wickham

Arriving at Los Carneros in Sonoma Valley for a tasting, one will notice the distinct Mexican culture seeping from the winery's pores. The tasting room itself is furnished with hand-carved furniture from Michoacan, Mexico, with photos of old Mexico on the walls and an ever-ready Robledo family member on hand for wine education or family stories. A long history of determination set Reynaldo on a journey from the mountains of Mexico to the hillsides of Sonoma, where humble beginnings as an immigrant sent him to become one of the most successful vineyard consultants and winery owners. This success is truly the Robledo family epic and a fine promise of the American dream.

WINE & FARE

Robledo Pinot Grigio, Lake County

Pair with roasted duck in tortillas, topped with habanero sauce.

Robledo Chardonnay, Los Carneros-Rancho Maria

Pair with crab empanadas filled with fruit pico de gallo and avocado-tomatillo salsa.

Robledo "El Rey" Cabernet Sauvignon, Lake County

Pair with filet mignon in wild mushroom-tequila cream sauce.

Tastings
Open by appointment only

Rodney Strong Vineyards

Healdsburg

For several years Rodney Strong danced his way around Paris. Trained at the School of American Ballet, Rod developed a taste for French wine and was determined to become a winemaker when his dancing career wound down. Coming back to America, he set out to compete with the great Bordeaux and Burgundy wines, specifically in Sonoma County.

In those early days, Sonoma County was agricultural, but had very few vineyards; it was mostly planted to fruit trees. However, shortly after he started in 1959, armed with a visionary approach to selecting sites where great grapes would grow, Rod purchased and planted in Sonoma County's best regions, Alexander Valley, Russian River Valley and Chalk Hill, which today are still home to the winery's best vineyards. By 1970 he had a new winery in Healdsburg. The site was originally a large prune-plum orchard, which Rod planted to pinot noir in the Russian River Valley—one of the first to do so. Among his other firsts, and in a push for quality wine that continues today, Rod produced the first single-vineyard Sonoma County cabernet sauvignon, Alexander's Crown, in 1974.

In 1979 Rod hired winemaker Rick Sayre. In the '80s the two met Tom Klein through business connections. Tom was fascinated with the business, and for the next decade, he absorbed facets of the winemaking industry, finally convincing his family to purchase the winery in 1989. Acquiring a winery that was well established as a high-quality producer of wines, Tom had some very specific ideas: "If you're going to own it, you want it to be special." Within each bottle, Tom wanted the pedigree of Sonoma County to shine through. For Rodney Strong Vineyards, "Place Matters" is manifest in each glass: wine that fully expresses Sonoma County terroir.

Top Left: Winery owner and chairman Tom Klein with winemaker Rick Sayre.
Photograph by Alan Campbell

Bottom Left: Rodney Strong Vineyards' tasting room is a Healdsburg must-see.
Photograph by Alan Campbell

Facing Page: Alexander's Crown Vineyard is a staple of Rodney Strong wines.
Photograph by Alan Campbell

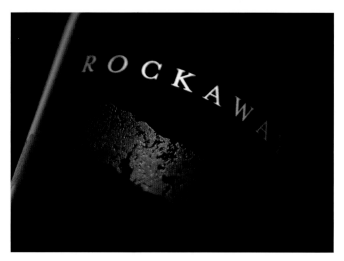

Top: Rodney Strong Vineyards' Rockaway Vineyard is in Geyserville.
Photograph by Alan Campbell

Bottom: Rockaway is a single-vineyard cabernet sauvignon and one of Rodney Strong's top selections.
Photograph by Alan Campbell

Top: Cloverdale is home to Rodney Strong Vineyards' Brothers Ridge Vineyard.
Photograph by Alan Campbell

Bottom: The winery-within-a-winery brings the finest winemaking equipment together with detail-oriented, artisan talent.
Photograph by Alan Campbell

Sonoma County's Alexander Valley is quickly rising in prestige with regard to cabernet sauvignon, and Rodney Strong Vineyards is part of a small group leading the way to this ultimate discovery. With three vineyards on eastern hillsides, each growing grapes for single-vineyard cabernets, tradition meets innovation as Tom and his winemaking team—Rick Sayre, Gary Patzwald and wine grower Doug McIlroy—craft distinctively rich, expressive wines. Each of these, Rockaway, Brothers Ridge and Alexander's Crown, is crafted in Rodney Strong Vineyards' winery-within-a-winery, where the group focuses on small lots of wine, hand-selected from sweet spots within each vineyard. With just under 1,000 total acres of vineyards throughout Sonoma County, Rodney Strong Vineyards is clearly dedicated to this county for the long haul. And, with the commitment to the region, so comes the winery's mission,

which, when you learn more about the company, leads to the obvious conclusion: Land stewardship is key. The winery conserves and protects the environment through sustainable and fish-friendly farming and the use of solar power—including one of the largest solar arrays in the wine industry.

Above: In a remarkably landscaped terrain, Rodney Strong Vineyards is compelling not only for its bottles, but also for its architecture.
Photograph by Alan Campbell

Facing Page: Winemaker Rick Sayre takes a sample from an oak barrel.
Photograph by Alan Campbell

The year 2009 marked three significant milestones for Rodney Strong Vineyards. The winery celebrated its 50-year anniversary, commemorated 30 years of Rick Sayre's winemaking and observed 20 years of Klein family ownership. With the numerous advances from Rodney Strong's winery-within-a-winery, these milestones point to a unique balance of consistency and a continual push for world-class quality, carrying the legacy of the founder into the second half of a century.

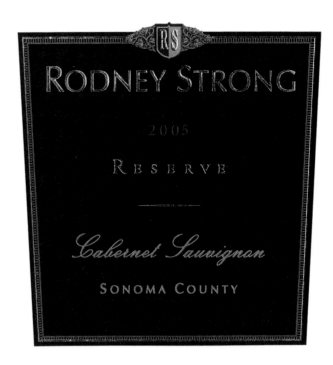

WINE & FARE

Cabernet Sauvignon Reserve, Sonoma County
(100% cabernet sauvignon)

Pair with porcini-crusted lamb loin.

Charlotte's Home Sauvignon Blanc
(100% sauvignon blanc)

Pair with fruit gazpacho.

Sonoma County Chardonnay
(100% chardonnay)

Pair with filet of halibut with orange, fennel and pepper salsa.

Tastings
Open to the public daily, year-round

Russian Hill Estate Winery

Windsor

Much of finding the perfect spot to start a winery is based on good fortune. Edward Gomez and Ellen Mack spent several years searching for the ideal place, a site that would give them full, hands-on control of wine production, from planting estate vineyards to building their own winery. From the onset, the couple knew that compromising on the site would be compromising on the wine, and this was unacceptable in their mission to produce excellent wines that are true expressions of the land. They also knew that pinot noir and syrah would thrive in the climate around the Russian River, and when they stumbled upon a location right in the heart of the Russian River Valley, their search ended, and Russian Hill Estate was born. Bringing in Patrick Melley—Ed's nephew—as head winemaker, the team began to develop the land for production.

Grapes have been planted in the area for nearly 200 years, and the region has become known as a producer of some of the best wines in the world. The fog that comes in from the ocean hangs here more than in other places, a cooling mechanism that is ideal to growing certain grape varieties, such as pinot noir and chardonnay. The effort in finding suitable land paid off as the grapes produced from Russian Hill's newly planted estate vineyards produced outstanding wines. A combination of excellent soils, good exposures and hands-on care of the vines has provided the perfect complement to the artisanal care the grapes receive once in the winery.

The site included a large house, complete with an ideal wine-tasting ballroom. An old Greek revival structure, the home was refurbished to the winery's purposes, yet the style

Top Left: The founding family of Russian Hill Estate is Edward Gomez, his wife, Ellen Mack, and their nephew, Patrick Melley.
Photograph by M.J. Wickham

Bottom Left: Winemaker Patrick Melley checks on the vineyard after harvest.
Photograph by M.J. Wickham

Facing Page: The pastoral setting at Russian Hill shows Ellen's Block Vineyard and a historic hop kiln in the distance from days when hops were commonly grown in Sonoma County.
Photograph by Warren H. W. White

Above Top: The Russian River Valley's fog creeps in during the early morning.
Photograph by Ellen Mack

Above Middle: The ballroom at Russian Hill Estate is a great place for dining.
Photograph by M.J. Wickham

Above Bottom: Guests enjoy the Russian Hill tasting-room patio with its spectacular views of the surrounding Russian River Valley.
Photograph by M.J. Wickham

Left: All roads lead to great wine at Russian Hill Estate.
Photograph by Ellen Mack

Facing Page: The essence of Russian Hill is captured in its Tara Vineyard Pinot Noir, favored by many dinner guests visiting the winery.
Photograph by M.J. Wickham

was maintained to keep in line with the history of the place. Now the rolling hills of the farming region are a great bucolic spot for picnics to soak in some of wine country's atmosphere.

Largely an estate winery, Russian Hill takes time to ensure that its wines are personable. This comes from control, beginning to end. Though during the first few years everyone did everything, roles are now more defined, with Patrick as winemaker, Ellen in the vineyards and in charge of general business, and Ed tinkering with bottling lines or reworking pumps—strictly a technical junky. Russian Hill Estate Winery is the result of people fulfilling their ambitions, and for the rest of us, a taste of, say, a Russian Hill pinot noir is certainly a palatable sampling of what Sonoma's wine country is all about.

RUSSIAN HILL

PINOT NOIR · SYRAH · CHARDONNAY
RUSSIAN RIVER VALLEY

ESTATE GROWN ❖ ESTATE BOTTLED

Wine & Fare

Gail Ann's Vineyard Chardonnay, Dutton Ranch

A refreshing, crisp chardonnay with flavors of citrus, green apple and pear that pairs exceptionally well with oysters, white fish and crab.

Estate Vineyards Pinot Noir

A robust pinot noir with a rich medley of berry, plum and earthy flavors that pairs well with roasted pork or grilled lamb.

Tara Vineyard Pinot Noir

An elegant pinot noir with classic Bing cherry and sassafras flavors that pairs beautifully with salmon and duck.

Top Block Syrah

Beautiful floral and spicy aromas enhance the plum and licorice flavors of this cool-climate syrah. It pairs exceptionally well with Indian or Moroccan cuisine as well as the classic pairings of roasted lamb or beef.

Tastings
Open to the public Thursday through Monday, year-round

Sbragia Family Vineyards

Geyserville

Maybe it was the resolute desire to stay connected to their homeland or perhaps even practicality that brought Ed Sbragia's relatives to beautiful Dry Creek Valley at the turn of the century. The valley's proximity to the Pacific Ocean, 20 miles west, and San Francisco Bay, more than 70 miles south, provides fog and a maritime influence that gives the valley a moderately cool climate similar to their Tuscan homeland. These influences would yield the type of grapes to which they were accustomed in their supple, balanced, flavorful Italian wines.

After the end of Prohibition, Ed's grandfather resettled in the Italian/Swiss colony in Asti to perfect his knowledge of winemaking and to purchase land. That knowledge passed to his son, Gino. In the 1940s, through his hard work and diligence, Gino bought land upon which to plant vineyards and build a home. It is that same house where Ed raised his family, and where his son Adam is now starting his family with his wife, Kathy, and baby daughter, Siena.

Although Ed had inherited a passion for winemaking, it didn't immediately reveal itself. After a bachelor's degree in chemistry poised him for a career in science, Ed changed his mind, receiving a master's in winemaking from the University of California. He began a successful and highly respected career with Beringer in 1976. In 2001 Ed created his own label, Sbragia Family Vineyards, making limited, individual lots of wine from grapes grown in select blocks of his favorite vineyards. He insisted that all of his wines be single-vineyard lots, made from Dry Creek, Napa, Sonoma and Alexander Valley fruit.

Top Left: From Warm Springs Dam, Sbragia Family Vineyards is ready for action.
Photograph by M.J. Wickham

Middle Left: The tasting Room and gift shop is a good place to start.
Photograph by M.J. Wickham

Bottom Left: Sbragia wines are prepared in the reserve tasting room.
Photograph by M.J. Wickham

Facing Page: Sbragia Family Vineyards enjoys a comfortable setting in Dry Creek Valley.
Photograph by M.J. Wickham

Each wine allows terroir to shine through. Four of the wines, including chardonnay, sauvignon blanc, merlot and zinfandel, are sourced from the Sbragia family estate vineyards. Having recently retired from his post as Beringer's Winemaster, Ed still maintains a relationship with Beringer as Winemaster Emeritus but gives his full-time attention to his family vineyards.

Ed once acknowledged that he prefers big wines with lots of flavor. The same could be said for how Ed lives and works: to the fullest and with lots of flavor to make it interesting. Working closely with what he loves most in his life—his family and the land—Ed realizes his good fortune. Adam has taken his place alongside his father as winemaker, while son, Kevin, works in the cellar during harvest. Adam's wife, Kathy, runs the vineyard's hospitality while both Ed's wife and daughter, Jane and Gina, respectively, help out in the tasting room where weddings and other special events are often hosted.

Top Left: The fog rolls into Dry Creek Valley, cooling the winery's fruit.
Photograph by M.J. Wickham

Middle Left: The private event space looks out from the terrace.
Photograph by M.J. Wickham

Bottom Left: The Sbragia family is Adam, Kathy, Siena, Gina, Kevin, Ed and Jane.
Photograph by Jeff Griffeath

Facing Page: Ed and Adam Sbragia take a break in the barreling room.
Photograph by M.J. Wickham

By creating a legacy for his children, Ed pays homage to his father every day. Growing up, Gino taught winemaking as a natural process; that all one needs for good wine is good land, good grapes and good techniques. Most importantly, Gino made Ed promise that he would care for his vineyards and eventually pass them on to his children. The vineyard around the winery was appropriately named La Promessa, as a reminder of the Sbragia covenant.

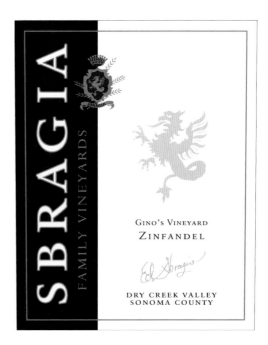

WINE & FARE

Gamble Ranch Chardonnay
Pair with gourmet mushroom soup with truffle oil.

Home Ranch Merlot
Pair with tortellini with Italian sausage.

Gino's Vineyard Zinfandel
Pair with pepper-crusted New York steak salad.

Cimarossa Vineyard Cabernet Sauvignon
Pair with fennel and Yukon Gold potato gratin.

Tastings
Open to the public daily, year-round

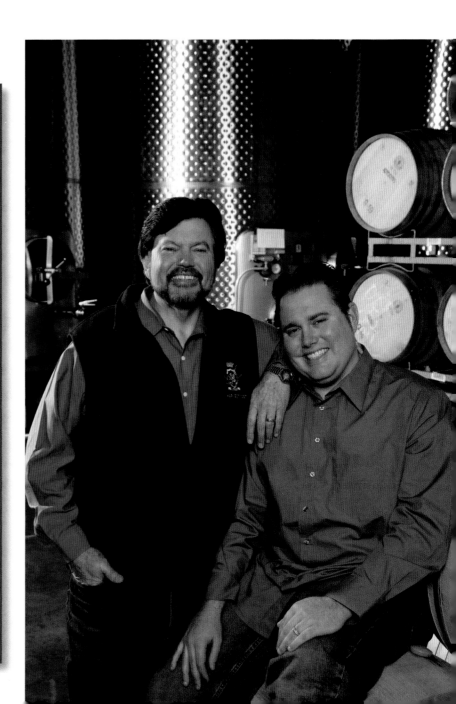

Seghesio Family Vineyards

Healdsburg

A hundred years ago the Seghesio family planted their first vines in Sonoma County. For the next century, the estate would grow to some 500 acres. From those fledgling roots in an industry that would take California by storm, Seghesio Family Vineyards takes the best of Old World Italian sensibilities and brings them to the New World. This is the epic tale of immigrant success in this country, a model for what desire, initiative and a little hard work can get. Still carrying the tradition, the Seghesios today are patrons of that drive, developing a wine program that cuts to the core of how the Italians treat wine.

Edoardo Seghesio left Piedmonte, Italy, for America in 1886. Though his family had worked in their own vineyards in Italy, Edoardo took this chance in America to work at the Italian Swiss Colony, gaining specialized knowledge in the craft of winemaking. He married Angela, the Colony manager's niece and a cook in the commissary. In 1895 the two planted the family's first zinfandel vines on what they called the Home Ranch. Business began to thrive as Edoardo and Angela developed a reputation for wines that best express the vineyards. In 1910 they added Italian varietals, including North America's now oldest planting of sangiovese.

Top Left: Old-vine zinfandel was planted on the Home Ranch in 1895 by Edoardo Seghesio.
Photograph by Richard Knapp

Bottom Left: The fruit of Seghesio's labor at harvest is a perfect zinfandel cluster.
Photograph by Richard Knapp

Facing Page: Seghesio's Home Ranch Vineyard stretches across Alexander Valley.
Photograph by M.J. Wickham

For the Seghesios, land influences the character of the wines from particular locations, such as Home Ranch, Cortina or Rockpile. These vineyard-designated wines have a strong sense of place. Seghesio Family Vineyards elicits this sense of place by ensuring a purity of fruit quality—indeed, they drop more crop than they harvest. Sustainable farming practices stimulate soil to guarantee uniqueness, with a little help from an ideal climate; the winery controls the stages of grape growing to produce wines of impeccable balance, clarity of fruit, concentration and complexity. This requires total knowledge of the vine's capabilities; and with most vineyards more than 30 years old, total vineyard erudition is easily achieved. Experience is certainly an invaluable commodity in the wine industry.

In Italy, wine has always been part of the table, and it is Seghesio Family Vineyards' goal to continue that tradition. Visitors to the estate suddenly find themselves in a culinary bliss not often found in this fast-paced country. Each Friday, Saturday and Sunday the winery hosts wine and food pairings for the public, aiming to share the passion and lifestyle with visitors. In fact, both food and wine served at the estate are 100-percent Sonoma County, securing distinctive, geographically based flavors.

Top Left: Seghesio's historic cellar in Healdsburg is Bonded Winery #56, dating to 1889.
Photograph by M.J. Wickham

Middle Left: The relaxed hospitality center exudes Seghesio's rich family history.
Photograph by M.J. Wickham

Bottom Left: Second, third and fourth generation family members passionately continue the family business into its second century.
Photograph by Richard Knapp

Facing Page: Seghesio's "Family Tables" allow weekend visitors the opportunity to experience the family's warmth and culinary skills as family recipes are paired with library wines.
Photograph by M.J. Wickham

With winemaking now in the hands of Ted Seghesio, the fourth generation of family winemakers, the winery still strives for uniqueness by displaying the uncommonly satisfying varietal flavors that do give a sense of place. Highly acclaimed over the last decades, Seghesio wines are a testament to the fact that intuition is an inherited trait.

WINE & FARE

Old Vine Zinfandel
(93% zinfandel, 7% petite sirah)

Pair with barbecue and spicy cuisine.

Home Ranch Zinfandel
(93% zinfandel, 5% petite sirah, 2% carignane)

Pair with beef, game and mascarpone cheese.

Sangiovese
(100% sangiovese)

Pair with red or mushroom-based sauces.

Tastings
Open to the public daily, year-round

Simi Winery

Healdsburg

Sometimes history means everything. For more than 130 years, Simi Winery has reigned in Sonoma County, growing grapes and crafting wines that showcase all of the qualities that make Sonoma County the remarkable Eden of American winemaking.

When the California Gold Rush hit in the mid-1800s, Giuseppe and Pietro Simi, brothers from Tuscany, came to conquer. By 1876 the two were producing wine out of San Francisco. There was something familiar, however, about Sonoma County—perhaps the rolling hills reminded them of Italy—and so the brothers set up a winemaking operation in Healdsburg. They built a stone cellar dug into the hillside to get at the natural insulation that the Earth provides. Success began to bubble, and when the brothers died, Giuseppe's daughter Isabelle, an 18-year-old, took over the winery. For the next 70 years, Isabelle orchestrated the winery's actions. She pushed Simi through Prohibition, which demolished most wineries, by storing much of the reserve for the inevitable repeal of the Act—she and her husband sold most of their vineyards to save the winery. After 15 years of dryness, Simi had a hoard of perfectly cellared wine, ready to drink. They even planted a redwood grove—which still stands—to celebrate the lawful flow of alcohol.

Since the beginning, Simi has enjoyed incredible growth, most notably in the last few decades. Winemaker Zelma Long came aboard in 1979, bringing a desire to modernize the winery's production. Around the same time, Simi began acquiring vineyards throughout Alexander Valley and Russian River Valley—including Landslide Vineyard.

Top Left: Vineyard director Tom Gore, winemaker Susan Lueker and general manager Steve Reeder stand in front of the winery.
Photograph by Avis Mandel

Middle Left: The historic railroad sign finds a new use at Simi Winery.
Photograph by Avis Mandel

Bottom Left: The pizza oven on the Landslide Terrace portends the approaching palate experience.
Photograph by Avis Mandel

Facing Page: Tours at Simi Winery start at the visitor center's stone fountain.
Photograph by M.J. Wickham

Top: The historic stone winery has a west side constructed by Asian railroad
workers and an east by Italian stonemasons.
Photograph by M.J. Wickham

Bottom: The stonework motif can be seen throughout the winery.
Photograph by M.J. Wickham

Top: The Red Fan Vineyard in the Alexander Valley exemplifies the rolling hillsides from which the wines spring.
Photograph by Avis Mandel

Bottom: Unique wood flooring pairs nicely with the oak barrels in the barrel room.
Photograph by M.J. Wickham

As a consultant, French winemaker Michel Rolland took Simi Winery as his first American client. Acclaim and critical success continued to pour. With the addition of a new visitor center and the nabbing of internationally recognized winemaker Steve Reeder as head winemaker in 2003, Simi Winery prepared itself to take on the new millennium with full force.

A timeline of this magnitude breeds expectations from the rest of us who drink Simi wines. Based on a Darwinian survival of tradition, Simi Winery continues to produce quality wines of the Simi style through cutting-edge innovation. For example, Simi purchased Goldfields Vineyard in Russian River Valley and planted hand-selected, original cuttings from some of the best and oldest vineyards in California, contributing to Simi Chardonnay's flavor diversity. As well, from Alexander Valley stems the winery's Bordeaux varietals, including its flagship Reserve Alexander Valley Cabernet Sauvignon and Landslide Vineyard Cabernet Sauvignon.

Sipping a Simi wine—if you have that much restraint— you discover some of the tradition, tasting the product of a pursuit for the finest vineyards, the finest grape-growing methods and the finest winemaking techniques. This is, however, an experience that can be had wherever you drink. But stepping into Simi Winery for a tasting offers a whole other experience. Recently Simi Winery created the Simi Landslide

Top Left: The Landslide Terrace is the hub of Simi's wine and fare program.
Photograph by M.J. Wickham

Middle Left: The hospitality center offers an alternative dining experience.
Photograph by M.J. Wickham

Bottom Left: Chef Eric Lee prepares one of his culinary masterworks.
Photograph by M.J. Wickham

Facing Page: Remarkable architecture and gorgeous landscaping greet visitors at the hospitality center.
Photograph by M.J. Wickham

Terrace, with waterfalls, a wood-burning pizza oven and a full Viking outdoor kitchen—making a total of three commercial kitchens for the winery. Simi's in-house chef heads an extensive food and wine program that will delight any palate.

With more than 700 acres of vines to choose from, Simi Winery takes care to produce wines that deliver the greatest expression from the soil and climate. Whether they come from the ancient landslide in Alexander Valley that changed the course of the Russian River, redistributing a variety of perfect wine soils, or the Goldfields Vineyard in the Russian River Valley that is the backbone of Simi's chardonnays, the wines that flow from Simi Winery are a definitive taste of California's Sonoma County wine country.

SIMI

2006
ALEXANDER VALLEY
CABERNET SAUVIGNON

Wine & Fare

Simi Alexander Valley Reserve Cabernet Sauvignon
Pair with ricotta gnocchi with duck Bolognese.

Sonoma County Chardonnay
Pair with halibut en papillote with orange-spice butter, couscous and broccolini.

Simi Sonoma Sauvignon Blanc
Pair with jerk duck with mango salsa, black beans and fried plantains.

Simi Sonoma County Merlot
Pair with short rib manicotti with paprika sauce.

Tastings
Open to the public daily, year-round

Sonoma–Cutrer Vineyards

Windsor

I f cabernet is the king of wines, then chardonnay is certainly the queen. As the wine industry began to develop in America, chardonnay was not as popular as its red counterparts—cabernet and zinfandel had a free-flowing fascination—but one grape-growing operation played a heavy role in turning the tide on whites. Sonoma–Cutrer Vineyards built its winery dedicated to "uni-varietal" wine production, with only chardonnay. This was a very unusual approach at the time, putting all your eggs in one basket, so to speak, but it proved hugely successful. Beginning with European influences on the wine-making process, Sonoma–Cutrer focused on producing chardonnay without compromise, by maintaining quality and desirability in each of its bottles of this liquid royalty.

In 1973 Sonoma–Cutrer Vineyards started growing several varieties of grapes, chardonnay among them. A selection of ideal vineyards in the Russian River Valley and Sonoma Coast appellations translated into remarkably adept growing conditions for chardonnay. These appellations are ideal for this varietal, with cool, foggy nights and warm days producing a longer growing season than in other parts of the county. As the '70s moved along, Sonoma–Cutrer Vineyards developed a very strong reputation for incredible chardonnay grapes, and the demand for them blossomed. It seemed only natural that the team would produce their own chardonnay, and by 1981, they produced their first vintage, with founding winemaker Bill Bonetti at the helm and Terry Adams as his assistant.

Top Left: Winemaker Terry Adams has been with Sonoma–Cutrer since its first vintage in 1981.
Photograph by Olaf Beckman

Bottom Left: Harvest-ready clusters hang on the vine.
Photograph by Olaf Beckman

Facing Page: The soil profile of Les Pierres Ranch is volcanic cobblestones.
Photograph by Tom Rider

Bill wanted to create chardonnay influenced by Old World methods, but with the benefit of modern technology. Bill adhered to the Burgundian philosophy that the wine is made in the vineyard, stressing the vines to produce small, intensely flavored grapes that are harvested by hand. He also insisted on gentle fruit handling, chilling the fruit in a specially designed cooling tunnel—the only one of its kind in the world—and hand-sorting the clusters on oscillating tables before being whole-cluster pressed, preserving the fruit and ensuring the finesse of the wine. Even the barrel cellar reflected state-of-the-art design with miles of built-in radiant heating and cooling tubes embedded in the floor and ceiling. Once the wine is in the barrel for fermentation and aging, it is hand-stirred and topped once a week, which adds body and complexity to the wine. The cellar was designed so that

the barrels do not sit on top of one another, enabling them to remain in place, accessible all throughout the winemaking process. The uncompromised method of sparing no cost to make great wine certainly became evident in the glass; the winery's sovereignty in the chardonnay field clearly held sway.

Above: The Cutrer Vineyard lies in the Russian River Valley.
Photograph by Olaf Beckman

Right: The barrel cellar was designed to provide space and access without moving the barrels during fermentation and aging.
Photograph by Teymoor Ghashghai

Facing Page Bottom: The clusters are put into one-third-ton bins to be taken to the winery.
Photograph by Olaf Beckman

Upon Bill's retirement in 1990, Terry Adams became the lead winemaker. Two dominating philosophies came out of this transition, the Grand Cru Program and a highly refined Barrel Program. The winery implemented these programs, as Terry says, to make wines that exemplify the character of the vineyards—that are fresh and lively—yet at the same time focused, balanced and structured. The Grand Cru Program exploits all the elements of terroir to their highest capacity. By reflecting the rigors of the French standard *Appellation d'Origine Controlée*, Sonoma–Cutrer Vineyards can classify precise blocks in the vineyard that meet Grand Cru requirements, such as soils, elevation, orientation, slope and climate. The result is excellence at its greatest echelon.

The refinement of the Barrel Program included hiring a *merrandier,* or forester, to select specific trees from various French forests to further enhance the flavors of the individual chardonnays. Once the trees are cut, the hand-split staves are seasoned for three years in the open air so that all imperfections in the wood are leached out. Old World coopers handcraft barrels that act as a frame for the wine, imparting understated flavors and aromas, soft and sensual. If the wine is to express its origins and its essence naturally, the winemaker must provide the environment and then step back and let the wine express itself and let nature have its say.

The critics have obviously noticed Sonoma–Cutrer Vineyards. *Wine & Spirits Magazine* listed the winery as producing the most-requested chardonnay

Top Left: The annual Make-a-Wish croquet tournament is a fundraising event that has taken place at Sonoma–Cutrer since 1990.
Photograph by Lauren Johnson

Bottom Left: Visitors celebrate the Derby Day Benefit with gourmet food and select Sonoma–Cutrer wine.
Photograph by Elizabeth Ghashghai

Facing Page: The winery looks out to the courts.
Photograph by Lauren Johnson

in fine restaurants for 18 out of the 20 years that they have done the survey. In this same poll, it was also declared the most popular of all varietals, red or white, and number one wine by the glass—a Triple Crown moment to be sure.

The future holds new promises. Recently the winery has begun producing a pinot noir from its 130 acres of pinot grapes. This wine is being produced to the same exacting standards applied to the chardonnay. With elegance and complexity, these wines are a testament to balance and continual character development. And for Sonoma–Cutrer Vineyards, tradition and discovery are the keys to astonishing wines.

ESTATE BOTTLED

SONOMA=CUTRER

RUSSIAN RIVER RANCHES

SONOMA COAST CHARDONNAY BOTTLED BY SONOMA-CUTRER VINEYARDS, WINDSOR, CA.

WINE & FARE

Russian River Ranches
Pair with tarragon chicken breasts with crab and asparagus.

Les Pierres
Pair with dayboat scallops in a creamy chardonnay sauce.

Pinot Noir
Pair with spring lamb tenderloin with dried cherries.

Tastings
Open by appointment only

Stonestreet Winery

Healdsburg

One place to begin the Stonestreet story would be 1989, with the winery's first vintage in Sonoma County. But the true starting point came much earlier, long before any human endeavor was involved. Three million years ago, in fact, when a volcano exploded and deposited a richness of rock, ash and minerals over what is now Napa and Sonoma counties. Over time, lava flow from that volcano created a mountain range between the two regions that today is called the Mayacamas Mountains—the rugged home to Stonestreet Winery and its vineyards on Alexander Mountain Estate.

Alexander Mountain Estate stands on the western ridge of the Mayacamas Mountains towering over the Alexander Valley below. High elevations, volcanically derived soils and cooling maritime breezes give the winery a unique location from which to pursue the labor of love that is mountain winegrowing. Of the 5,400 acres that make up the estate, only 774 are planted to grapes made of 400 individual vineyard blocks, planted at elevations that range from 400 to 2,400 feet above sea level. This incredible terrain produces an intricate puzzle of peaks, valleys and ridges with a broad spectrum of facings and aspects.

The mountain conditions are difficult to farm and labor intensive, as each block requires a personal, hands-on approach. The mountain conditions are so different that grapes on the same vine ripen at different times, leading to different dates of harvest. It takes an artisan approach to master these complexities and produce wines of elegance and concentration that reflect the true essence and beauty of this unique location. Cabernet sauvignon and chardonnay shine the brightest under these conditions, and Stonestreet's entire winemaking philosophy, the pinnacle of which is showcased by the single-vineyard bottlings, is oriented to expressing the purest sense of place.

Left: Stonestreet Winery is located on Highway 128 just outside of the town of Healdsburg. The Stonestreet tasting room offers limited-production wines that are only available through the winery.
Photographs by M.J. Wickham

Facing Page: Stonestreet's vineyards on Alexander Mountain Estate range from 400 to 2,400 feet above sea level.
Photograph by M.J. Wickham

Above Top: There is a postcard vista from the patio of the Stonestreet tasting room.
Photograph by M.J. Wickham

Above Middle: The rose arbor is where several of Stonestreet's private events are held.
Photograph by M.J. Wickham

Above Bottom: Only one-fifth of the 5,400 acres on Alexander Mountain Estate has been planted to vine.
Photograph by M.J. Wickham

Left: The terrain on Alexander Mountain Estate creates a puzzle of peaks, valleys and ridges.
Photograph by M.J. Wickham

Located just outside of Healdsburg, Stonestreet Winery is immersed in—and inspired by—its wild and remote surroundings. At 5,400 acres, the estate is vast. But Stonestreet believes in respectful cohabitation with this remarkable land and has only planted one-fifth to vine. The remaining terrain retains its natural biodiversity and abounds with streambeds, redwoods and ancient oak trees, providing habitat to cougars, owls and wild boar.

Above: The cabernet sauvignon Block 430C is at 2,000 feet above sea level.
Photograph by M.J. Wickham

Facing Page: Garden walks through the rose arbor make for perfect afternoons.
Photograph by M.J. Wickham

Stonestreet Winery and Alexander Mountain Estate can be experienced first hand by taking part in a Mountain Excursion—a tour of Alexander Mountain Estate in which visitors experience the sights, sounds and smells that define the estate. The Mountain Excursion also includes a picnic lunch on Alexander Mountain Estate followed by a tasting of the single-vineyard selections.

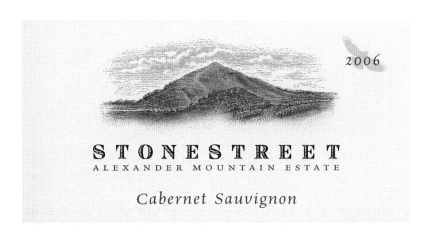

WINE & FARE

Stonestreet Alexander Valley Chardonnay

*Pair with pasta with white sauce, light seafood
or pork tenderloin.*

Stonestreet Fifth Ridge—Red Wine Blend

*Pair with "medium" red meats such as lamb, pork or
pheasant, or with red-sauced pastas or vegetarian lasagna.*

Alexander Valley Cabernet Sauvignon

*Pair with grilled steak with root vegetables or flavorful cheeses
including aged cheddar, Parmesan or fontina.*

Stonestreet Christopher's Cabernet Sauvignon

Pair with filet with crumbled bleu cheese or duck confit.

Tastings
Open to the public daily, year-round

Stryker Sonoma Winery

Geyserville

For some, risk may be an element that deters an innovative approach to winemaking. For others, the innovative approach may be worth the effort. Stryker Sonoma Winery set out with bold measures: The wine that its team loves to drink is worth every effort, despite the level of risk. These bold, forward-style wines continue to pay off, for the following of appreciative drinkers shows the exacting strengths in Stryker Sonoma's methodology. Stryker Sonoma wines are truly handcrafted, making use of both Old World methods and the judicious integration of modern tools designed to allow for gentler handling of both fruit and wine.

Youthful enthusiasm and a tireless dedication to the pursuit of quality and pleasure guides Stryker Sonoma's winemaking style. A slightly irreverent attitude with respect to the traditional methods of producing and marketing wine leads this group of fun-loving winemakers—the cold bottle of sparkly after the first harvest sets the mood. The team goes to considerable expense to grow and produce clean, balanced wines that are fully extracted and rich in complexity and that comprise depth of character. These wines are enjoyable in their youth, but also rewarding to those with patience.

Top Left & Facing Page: The winery is harmoniously woven into the natural setting; exterior and interior form an organic whole.
Photographs by M.J. Wickham

Bottom Left: Hard work, attention to detail and enjoyment go into every wine that Tim Hardin crafts.
Photograph by M.J. Wickham

Stryker Sonoma focuses its mission around the Bordelaise varietals. There is, however, a keen interest in zinfandel and chardonnay, because of the ideal climatic conditions in the terrific spot in California. Nestled on a knoll, Stryker Sonoma's location typifies the peaceful, serene beauty of the Alexander Valley. This quality, along with the famous cabernets, drew founders and partners Pat Stryker and Craig MacDonald to the area in 1999. Along with winemaker Tim Hardin, the winery set about to break molds of production. The winery's design was to integrate the production facility with the visitors center, thereby offering visitors a unique educational opportunity of a behind-the-scenes look into a small working winery.

Stryker makes many different wines with a number of varietals, but the annual production is limited to 7,000 cases, consisting of many small lots ranging in size from 100 to 400 cases each. The Stryker 2002 Monte

Rosso Vineyard Cabernet Sauvignon is made with grapes from the famous property on the Sonoma side of the Mayacamas Mountains. The Monte Rosso vineyard is named after its conspicuous red soil, and it sits at 1,000 feet above the Sonoma Valley floor. In addition to Monte Rosso Cabernet, Stryker Sonoma makes several other cabernets including Rockpile Cabernet, Two Moon Vineyard from Dry Creek Valley, Speedy Creek Vineyard from Knights Valley, Estate Vineyard from Alexander Valley and Sonoma County Reserve Cabernet Sauvignon.

Above: Inspired by mid-century modern American architecture, the winery uses traditional forms and materials in new ways.
Photograph by M.J. Wickham

Facing Page: Stryker Sonoma's philosophy is reflected in both in the design of the winery and the team's approach to winemaking: bold but thoughtful, a blend of traditional and modern, efficient yet lively and spirited.
Photograph by M.J. Wickham

With more than 500 wineries in the surrounding counties, each has to push for distinction. While perhaps being one of the most sought-after destinations for weddings in wine country, Stryker Sonoma recently won a Best Winery Tasting Room award—a competition in which contenders cannot enter, but rather, rely completely on the consumer's recommendations. Also the winner of the 2002 Architectural Design Award for Northern California, Stryker Sonoma Winery has set the record for the most gold and silver medals ever won by a single winery at the Sonoma County Harvest Fair—a total of 22. The risk has certainly been worth the effort.

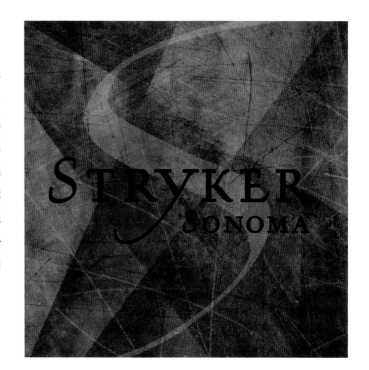

Wine & Fare

"Oz" Alexander Valley Zinfandel
Pair with dry-rub baby back ribs.

Rockpile Vineyard Petit Verdot
Pair with wagyu beef.

Tastings
Open to the public daily, year-round

Vérité Winery

Healdsburg

The confluence of Old World thinking and New World fruit is relatively new to California. The winemaking at Vérité Winery is a bridge between these two worlds, the crossing of which has been led by Pierre Seillan, one of France's most highly regarded and respected vignerons, since 1998.

Pierre's philosophy of farming vineyards involves assessing all of the factors that impact the fruit quality and determining specifically which rootstocks, varieties and clones will produce at the highest quality given the soils' aspect and micro-climate factors involved. By looking at the vineyard and farming in this manner, he creates small blocks within the vineyard, some comprised of only a few rows of grapes, each representing the ideal expression of the variety planted there. Pierre calls these blocks "micro-crus." The micro-crus are farmed, harvested and vinified separately. From the cabernet sauvignon that emerges from the volcanic soil of Alexander Valley, to merlot in the maritime region of Bennett Valley or gravelly Knights Valley, the grapes that Pierre amasses are true expressions of their soil and perfect components for masterfully blended wines.

Top Left: From the grapes ... Vigneron Winemaster Pierre Seillan says that great wine starts in the vineyard, with careful farming and a philosophy of "micro-crus."
Photograph by Jerome Baudoin

Bottom Left: ... to the glass: Carefully processing all of the fruit and constantly tasting during vinification ensures the highest-quality juice goes into the wines.
Photograph by M.J. Wickham

Facing Page: The diverse and varied terrain of Alexander Mountain Estate, Alexander Valley, contains many unique soil types and terroirs at high elevations.
Photograph by M.J. Wickham

Above Top: Jackson Park Vineyard, Bennett Valley, was planted by Pierre several years ago and produces great merlot grapes.
Photograph by George Rose

Above Middle: The oak terrace that extends out from the tasting room is a great place to view the estate's vineyards.
Photograph by M.J. Wickham

Above Bottom: A special private lunch and tasting on the terrace is a unique treat with pairings created by Chef Taki Laliotitis.
Photograph by M.J. Wickham

Left: The vineyards of Vérité Vale, Chalk Hill, extend out behind the winery and tasting room, which surround the pond.
Photograph by M.J. Wickham

Vérité Winery produces three wines, each an expression of a Bordeaux variety, crafted by Pierre to highlight that particular variety. La Muse is French for inspiration, and Vérité Winery's version is absolutely something to muse over—a primarily merlot blend culled from the hillsides of the Mayacamas Mountains. La Joie (Joy) is a joyously deep, dark, cabernet sauvignon-based wine. Le Désir (Desire) is Pierre's expression of cabernet franc and is a testimony to full-bodied richness.

All of the wines are aged in French oak as an undetectable addition to the wines' architecture, resulting in bottles that age wonderfully for

decades. Through each of these wines, the consumer will experience a layering of components not often found on this side of the globe. The balance, complexity and depth of flavor in each are a testament not only to the quality of the vineyards from which Pierre harvests, but also to his ability as a vigneron and blender. From handpicking and sorting the berries, to aging the wine in French oak barrels, the Vérité team

Above: Experience French hospitality in Sonoma, as Vigneron Winemaster Pierre Seillan and his wife Monique are always ready to greet visitors to a formal seated tasting in the tasting room.
Photograph by M.J. Wickham

Facing Page: The wines of Vérité are great for cellar aging as well as decanting to enjoy with a range of food pairings.
Photograph by M.J. Wickham

takes calculated steps to develop varieties that drink great now as well as age alongside the best Bordeaux wines. Vérité wines have received outstanding recognition as some of the finest wines produced in the world, revealing ingenious blends and the boundless harvest of Sonoma's diverse terroir.

VÉRITÉ

La Muse

2004

SONOMA COUNTY RED WINE

WINE & FARE

La Muse
Pair with grilled salmon, rack of lamb or Gruyère cheese.

La Joie
*Pair with beef tenderloin, filet mignon, venison
or a Camembert or Brie cheese.*

Le Désir
*Pair with duck cassoulet, roasted rabbit, monkfish, truffles,
Comté or Petit Basque cheese.*

Tastings
Open by appointment only

Viansa Italian Village & Winery

Sonoma

Italy's Old World traditions gain our reverence, for the love of wine, food and country pleasures sing to our inner selves. The experience of that delightful, Mediterranean lifestyle is often lost these days, yet when we relax on a verdant hilltop and enjoy Italian and Californian wines paired with great food and friends, it feels natural, as things should be.

Set at the gateway to Sonoma Valley, Viansa Italian Village & Winery celebrates the fundamental nature of Italy in Sonoma Valley. The experience at Viansa is holistic. In tandem, the village and winery create a destination unlike anything outside of Tuscany. This is wine country at its greatest potential, for the journey through the village is an enchanting trip. Viansa develops its Italian identity—from its architecture, ornate grounds, garden, vineyard and olive groves to the true flavors of Italy: the wines, the food, the gifts and accoutrements, plus the culture of festivals, music and art.

The village delivers the ultimate Italian-Californian spirit. Viansa's villa crowns a vine-covered hilltop, recalling the quaint nature of picturesque Tuscan country estates. Here, family and friends gather seeking good wines, good food and good fun. The cultural immersion is so encompassing that you almost forget why you came in the first-place, which, of course, was for the Italian wines crafted in Sonoma from authentic Italian varieties, such as sangiovese, aleatico and primitivo, as well as a full assortment of California classics, such as cabernet sauvignon, chardonnay, merlot and zinfandel.

Top Left: Viansa's commanding hilltop location showcases vineyard, valley and mountain views. It's quite a site for everything from luxurious celebrations to simple picnics.
Photograph by JayKellyPhoto.com

Bottom Left: The winery's Tuscan Club members receive monthly selections of Italian and Sonoma classic wines paired with unique recipes and special ingredients.
Photograph courtesy of Viansa Italian Village & Winery

Facing Page: The wetlands preserve is home to more than 170 species of birds and countless wildlife. As many as 10,000 waterfowl have been counted in a single day.
Photograph by Doug Conaway

The tile-roofed Tuscan-style villa—adorned with hand-painted beams, Italian marble, engaging frescoes and massive windows and doors—was designed after an Italian monastery. Sitting atop the piazza that is Viansa, the villa serves as host to many multidimensional happenings, from public gatherings with music and art, to more private affairs, such as weddings and business and social events. There are eight distinct venues for private events that can accommodate groups from 10 to 220 beautifully.

The panoramic views of the neighboring and distant mountains are nothing short of spectacular and function as a terrific backdrop to all wine-country events. Since most wineries are settled in valleys, Viansa's iconic vantage point showcasing 360-degree views is an incredible rarity.

One of the most fascinating elements of Viansa is the 90-acre wetlands preserve. This sacred space thrives under Viansa's stewardship. Throughout the year the winery tends to wetlands restoration, welcoming canvasback ducks, great blue herons and other birds migrating along the Pacific Flyway—more than 170 species of birds have been sighted on these restored coastal wetlands, including Canadian geese, egrets, owls, hawks and, occasionally, a rare tundra swan. Taking part in the conservation of the reserve reflects the core value of Viansa, and for the rest of us, calls to our desire to preserve the land from which we came.

Top Right: The Italian marketplace has just the right ingredients for fun food pairings, hilltop picnics or festive meals at home.
Photograph by M.J. Wickham

Bottom Right: Housing Viansa's rare vintages and most exclusive wines, the Enoteca is a magical setting for private tastings.
Photograph courtesy of Viansa Italian Village & Winery

Facing Page Top: The villa was designed after an Italian monastery.
Photograph courtesy of Viansa Italian Village & Winery

Facing Page Bottom: Viansa sits majestically on a vine-covered hilltop at the gateway to Sonoma Valley. The villa's grand courtyard is open to visitors and used year-round for special events.
Photographs courtesy of Viansa Italian Village & Winery

Taking the wine-country experience to new heights is Viansa's ragion d'essere. The Tuscan Club, for example, hosts myriad activities and events for its 10,000-plus members throughout the year. The winemaker is typically on hand to deliver insider information on the intricate details of creating Viansa's wine program. Because food and wine pairings are such an intrinsic part of the Italian culinary experience, Viansa's chef prepares special lunches that may pair the two with careful consideration of the subtle nuances of each variety. Artisan cheeses often make appearances, and Viansa always pushes for adventuresome pairings to integrate discovery on unfamiliar planes. One of the big draws, however, is that Tuscan Club members not only get custom recipes with their monthly offerings, they also get exclusive ingredients with their delivery that really develop the essence of the meal.

It is not unusual for people to spend more than a few hours visiting Viansa because there is so much to see and do. Tours of the expansive grounds and villa are available on any day of the week. Viansa wines continually receive notable medals and accolades, and visitors get to see why when they enter the Italian marketplace and tasting room. The deli features a wide array of artisan cheeses, meats, salads, olives, peppers and fresh fruits—the makings of a tasty

Top Left: Reflecting a hilltop village in Tuscany, Viansa's manicured grounds and vibrant piazza celebrate the traditions of Italy in Sonoma Valley.
Photograph courtesy of Viansa Italian Village & Winery

Middle & Bottom Left: Panoramic views from a host of indoor and outdoor venues make events memorable. Fairy tale weddings— from intimately sized to 220 guests—have become a particular source of pride.
Photographs courtesy of Viansa Italian Village & Winery

Facing Page: The winemaker and chef create convivial lunches and dinners with inspired food and wine parings. With 18 Italian and 13 Sonoma classic wines to pair, there's always something new to delight Tuscan Club members and guests.
Photograph by M.J. Wickham

Previous Pages: Located 30 feet underground and filled with oak wine barrels, the cellar is an enchanting setting for formal candlelit dinners or festive gatherings of family and friends.
Photograph by M.J. Wickham

food-pairing experience and a wine-country picnic. Viansa's in-house chef prepares its delicacies from scratch. The select products as well as exclusive Viansa brand food and condiments, crafts and accessories all make distinctive gifts.

Exclusive, artisan, local. Whether one enjoys the wide array of wines—including some 18 Italian varieties and 13 Sonoma Valley classics—or the vast fare from the Italian marketplace, Viansa is a savory journey to a great wine-country destination. With exceptional wines, inspired foods, traditional activities and events, Viansa celebrates the essence of Italy to be enjoyed time and time again.

Italian Village and Winery
A festival of wine, food and country pleasures.

WINE & FARE

"Cento per Cento" Estate Chardonnay
Pairs wonderfully with Viansa's "salmon and shrimp cakes" or "orchiette with saffron and cauliflower."

"Farneta" Carneros Primitivo
Pair with herb-rubbed steaks or plum-glazed ribs—a perfect match for summer barbecue fare—as well as classic Italian dishes such as eggplant Parmesan and sausages with roasted peppers.

"Augusto" Sonoma Mountain Barbera
Pair with barbecue fare with a maple sauce or grilled pork tenderloin and lasagna. But also delightful by itself.

"Pierina" Estate Vernaccia
Pairs nicely with seafood linguine, crab cakes, grilled swordfish and halibut.

Tastings
Open to the public daily, year-round

Wilson Winery

Healdsburg

At first, Wilson Winery's old tin barn on Dry Creek Road appears unassuming. But this century-old building is a perfect token of Americana, like something out of a Steinbeck novel. Wilson Winery was born here, in a structure rooted deep in American history and located in one of the most remarkable scenes in Dry Creek Valley. The postcard vistas from the back of this barn are the quintessence of Sonoma County, the soul of wine country. And for Ken and Diane Wilson, this spot was the deciding factor in their immersion into the winemaking industry. The old barn became an essential metaphor for restoration, for stewardship and for rebirth—all under the baton of passionate winemaking.

The Wilsons are devoted to things they most value—family, friends and the Dry Creek Valley. Beginning in the early 1980s, Diane and Ken started as grape growers. Dry Creek Valley, for the two, had the perfect mix of oaks, vineyards and views, and over the next decade, the couple developed some 220 acres of zinfandel, cabernet sauvignon, cabernet franc, syrah and merlot grapes. These vineyards would epitomize earth-friendly, sustainable farming and would become extensions of the idea of family. Strong family ties are seen everywhere; in fact, each of the three daughters—Tori, Sawyer and Sydney— have namesake vineyards—even the grandparents and the dog get vineyard names. Once firmly established as one of Dry Creek Valley's top growers, it was time to fulfill their dream of making wine.

Left: Combining her passion for cooking with her educational background in biochemistry, winemaker Diane Wilson has developed a style of winemaking that is equal parts of science, passion and art.
Photographs by M.J. Wickham

Facing Page: Each of the estate vineyards is named for a member of the Wilson family.
Photograph by M.J. Wickham

As winemaker, Diane produces artisan wines of exceptional depth and intensity. Diane strives to foster exuberant wines boasting intense flavors, richly textured with structure and balance, that reflect the particular qualities of each vineyard site. Making wine is a balance, requiring a dose of experience and intuition, a dash of discipline and a lust for discovery. Wilson Winery's first vintage, a 1994 cabernet sauvignon that sprang from Sydney Vineyard, won best in class and a gold medal.

Each year, Wilson Winery produces 5,000 cases of red wine, each bottle of which speaks to Diane and Ken's passion. With a growing list of gold medals and 90-plus ratings—including Sonoma County Harvest Fair's

Red Wine Sweepstakes Award two years in a row—Wilson Winery wines sell out very quickly. But friends and family still tie the winery together. With the old barn refurbished, the winery is now a hotspot for soaking in the beauty of the county, to make wine the experience that it should be. Ken and Diane also founded the Children of Vineyard Worker's Scholarship, allowing for an education that might otherwise be unaffordable.

Above: The Wilsons farm 220 acres of hillside vineyards in the Dry Creek Valley appellation.
Photograph by M.J. Wickham

Facing Page: For visitors who can't seem to pull themselves away from the property and those who haven't yet made the trip, each of Wilson's wine clubs offers a great way to connect with the wines and the people who create them.
Photograph by M.J. Wickham

Wilson Winery practices the Robert Frost approach to production: Patience with a willingness to take risks and choosing the road less traveled are the stuff of legacies. The family's commitment to this philosophy and to the relentless pursuit of quality encompasses the essence of Dry Creek Valley.

Wine & Fare

2005 Sydney Vineyard Reserve Cabernet

Pair with grilled rib eye and sautéed Brussels sprouts with pecans and Parmesan cheese.

2006 Sawyer Vineyard Zinfandel

Pair with meatballs with pomegranate currant sauce served with endive salad with goat cheese and walnuts.

2006 Carl's Vineyard Zinfandel

Pair with ham and Jarlsberg strata and a fresh greens salad with blood orange slices topped with balsamic dressing.

Tastings
Open to the public daily, year-round

Taylor Lombardo Architects, page 294

Seguin Moreau Napa Cooperage, page 290

Behind the Wines

Landmark Label Manufacturing, Inc.

Fremont

Bridging the visions of winemakers since 1986, Landmark Label Manufacturing produces stunning custom labels, illustrating the passion and creativity inherent in all winemaking.

Landmark Label is where artistry meets technology. Landmark's skilled graphic artists and pressmen take great pride in each label produced and recognize that labels are masterpieces conveying the winemakers' devotion, elegance and imagination, depicting the grand stories of wineries, families and legacies. Wine labels produced today are essential in winery branding—putting a face with the wine—and entire campaigns are often based around their design. Great labels attract, persuade and ultimately influence purchasing behavior.

Landmark's extensive press capabilities and its willingness to take on new projects, regardless of size, confirm the fundamental principle at Landmark Label Manufacturing: They love a challenge.

Complete client satisfaction is Landmark's top priority. Landmark's people are attentive, excellent communicators and problem-solvers, and go to great lengths to understand the specialized needs of each client. Whether working side by side with the vintners at Landmark or on the bottling line at the winery, Landmark overcomes objectives, gains knowledge from each obstacle, and continually evolves its practices, thus shifting the paradigm of the industry.

Top Right: One of Landmark's talented pressmen setting up his Flexo press for the Biltmore Estate Winery Chardonnay label.
Photograph by Elpidio Felipe

Middle Right: The Biltmore Estate Winery 2008 Chardonnay label comes off the press. Notice the removal of the matrix.
Photograph by Elpidio Felipe

Bottom Right: A collage of Biltmore Estate Winery labels shows a wide range of possibilities.
Photograph by Bob Albers

Facing Page: The Biltmore Reserve Russian River Valley Pinot Noir label depicts a china plate set on an embossed table cloth, complete with a Biltmore Reserve place card.
Photograph by Bob Albers

Seguin Moreau Napa Cooperage

Napa

For a thousand years wine barrels were looked upon just as containers, a way to keep the wine from soaking into the ground. These fruits of the cooper's trade, however, were and are the image of wine—the romance of winemaking lies in the cellars where tall stacks of aged barrels hold quaffable charms. But not until fairly recent breakthroughs in technology did cooperages start to understand the effects that the wood has as wine swirls around in the belly of the barrel. Digging behind the romance, Seguin Moreau Napa Cooperage was the first to understand the interaction of wine and wood; and with a lot of strategy and a lot of science, the cooperage uses that romance to stoke the fire, as it were.

Seguin and Moreau began as separate cooperages, with Moreau founding in 1838 and Seguin in 1870. Located in the Charente region of France, near Bordeaux, the cooperages were in cognac territory, making barrels nearly exclusively for the cognac industry. In 1958 Remy Martin bought the two cooperages and combined them for its own purposes. Cognac had a great renaissance in the 1970s; but the demand for high-quality wine soon accelerated as well. Seeing a new opportunity, Seguin Moreau started producing barrels for wine, and an aggressive R&D campaign began. Very quickly it became evident to Seguin Moreau that wood types were of singular import.

Top Right: The cooperage, located in Napa, is the premier California creator of French oak barrels.
Photograph by M.J. Wickham

Middle Right: Fire and water are used to soften the wood, allowing the staves to be bent into shape.
Photograph by M.J. Wickham

Bottom Right: After shaping and toasting, barrels wait to be finished so that their aesthetic beauty equals the functional quality.
Photograph by M.J. Wickham

Facing Page: The first firing gives the barrel its shape. Upending the barrels, each end is hooped in turn, giving a blossomed-rose shape to the staves.
Photograph by M.J. Wickham

From this springboard, 25 years ago, Seguin Moreau became pioneers in wood science. A good barrel selection can offer structure and aromas of vastly varying degrees; the type of wood, the tightness of the grain and the level of toasting are each an important element in barrel selection. Part of the cooperage's technological prowess led to a method of wood seasoning called proactive maturation: The maturation of wood is monitored and controlled, based on meteorological data. Wood is carefully seasoned in Missouri and France, under the same principles in both places but with some differing details, according to oak species.

Because of the potentially infinite variety of barrels, almost every order that Seguin Moreau receives is custom made. To get to the exacting specifications of the winemaker the cooperage needed to have direct access on a daily basis; hence, Seguin Moreau became the first to produce French oak out of Napa for California wineries. The cooperage looks for understanding in their product, whether it is the effect on wine or on the Earth—Seguin Moreau was the first cooperage to be certified by PEFC for its work with sustainable forest management. This reputation has resulted in heavy use—a dip into a Seguin Moreau barrel will draw out a glass of any of a number of the world's greatest wines.

Left: Coopering is a true combination of art and craft; years of training are the vital requisite for making great barrels.
Photograph by M.J. Wickham

Facing Page Top: The architecture of Seguin Moreau is specifically designed to integrate with the Napa Valley scenery.
Photograph by M.J. Wickham

Facing Page Bottom Left: The second firing creates the flavors that will work their way into the wines.
Photograph by M.J. Wickham

Facing Page Bottom Right: Seguin Moreau is the leader in French oak barrels, and the cooperage's crest can found on the barrels of the most prestigious wines in the world.
Photograph by M.J. Wickham

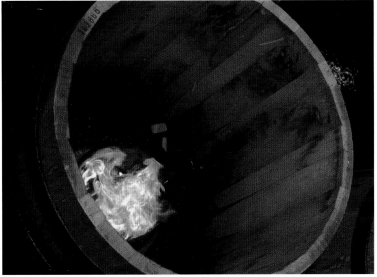

Taylor Lombardo Architects

San Francisco

A winery is a unique building type, one that must seamlessly combine streamlined efficiency with an evocative, even romantic environment.

Taylor Lombardo Architects specializes in the design of wineries of all types and sizes, and during the last two decades, the firm has cultivated an extensive knowledge of the winemaking process. The facilities designed by the firm utilize inventive layouts to make the production process as efficient as possible. Additionally, the designs incorporate the latest in environmentally friendly technologies and sustainable materials.

A winery building acts as a laboratory for winemakers as well as a hospitality venue for guests. While a winery is by definition an agricultural building type, there is much room for innovation in the design process. Working closely with the owners, Taylor Lombardo Architects defines the winery's program elements, which in turn helps inform the basic plan of the buildings.

During the design process, careful thought is given to the relationship and flow of spaces as well as the connection of the building to its site. The end result is a beautifully proportioned production facility that is flexible enough to function as an elegant event space.

Top Right: Freestone Winery is a state-of-the-art, gravity-flow production facility that produces organic pinot noir.
Photograph by M.J. Wickham

Middle Right: The wine library, built of steel and glass with reclaimed oak wood racks, provides temperature-controlled storage for an exclusive wine collection.
Photograph by Odessa Schneider

Bottom Right: Located in the city of Cloverdale, Peay Winery was designed in an agricultural barn vernacular.
Photograph by Jason Liske

Facing Page: This private residential wine cave affords a simple yet elegant space for the owners to entertain friends.
Photograph by M.J. Wickham

Spectacular Wineries of Sonoma County

Sonoma County Team

Regional Publisher: Kathryn Newell

Regional Publisher: Carla Bowers

Senior Designer: Emily A. Kattan

Editor: Daniel Reid

Production Coordinator: Laura Greenwood

Production Coordinator: Drea Williams

Headquarters Team

Publisher: Brian G. Carabet

Publisher: John A. Shand

Executive Publisher: Phil Reavis

Director of Development & Design: Beth Benton Buckley

Director of Book Marketing & Distribution: Julia Hoover

Publication Manager: Lauren B. Castelli

Graphic Designer: Kendall Muellner

Graphic Designer: Ashley Rodges

Editorial Development Specialist: Elizabeth Gionta

Managing Editor: Rosalie Z. Wilson

Editor: Anita M. Kasmar

Editor: Michael C. McConnell

Managing Production Coordinator: Kristy Randall

Traffic Coordinator: Meghan Anderson

Administrative Manager: Carol Kendall

Administrative Assistant: Beverly Smith

Client Support Coordinator: Amanda Mathers

PANACHE PARTNERS, LLC

CORPORATE HEADQUARTERS

1424 Gables Court

Plano, TX 75075

469.246.6060

www.panache.com

A. Rafanelli Winery
4685 West Dry Creek Road
Healdsburg, CA 95448
707.433.1385
www.arafanelliwinery.com

Audelssa Estate Winery
13647 Arnold Drive
Glen Ellen, CA 95442
707.933.8514
www.audelssa.com

Benziger Family Winery
1883 London Ranch Road
Glen Ellen, CA 95442
888.490.2739
www.benziger.com

C. Donatiello Winery
4035 Westside Road
Healdsburg, CA 95448
707.431.4442
www.cdonatiello.com

Charles Creek Vineyards
483 First Street West
Sonoma, CA 95476
707.935.3848
www.charlescreek.com

Cline Cellars
24737 Arnold Drive
Sonoma, CA 95476
707.940.4030
www.clinecellars.com

Davis Bynum Winery
8075 Westside Road
Healdsburg, CA 95448
866.442.7547
www.davisbynum.com

Deerfield Ranch Winery
10200 Sonoma Highway
Kenwood, CA 95452
707.833.5215
www.deerfieldranch.com

deLorimier Vineyards & Winery
2001 Highway 128
Geyserville, CA 95441
800.546.7718
www.delorimierwinery.com

Dutcher Crossing Winery
8533 Dry Creek Road
Healdsburg, CA 95448
707.431.2700
www.dutchercrossingwinery.com

Ferrari-Carano Vineyards and Winery
8761 Dry Creek Road
Healdsburg, CA 95448
800.831.0381
707.433.6700
www.ferrari-carano.com

Fisher Vineyards
6200 St. Helena Road
Mayacamas Mountains, CA 95404
707.539.7511
www.fishervineyards.com

Foppiano Vineyards
12707 Old Redwood Highway
Healdsburg, CA 95448
707.433.7272
www.foppiano.com

Freeman Vineyard & Winery
P.O. Box 1556
Sebastopol, CA 95472
707.823.6937
www.freemanwinery.com

Freestone Vineyards
12747 El Camino Bodega
Freestone, CA 95472
707.874.1010
www.freestonevineyards.com

Gary Farrell Vineyards & Winery
10701 Westside Road
Healdsburg, CA 95448
707.473.2909
www.garyfarrellwines.com

Hanzell Vineyards
18596 Lomita Avenue
Sonoma, CA 95476
707.996.3860
www.hanzell.com

Hartford Family Winery
8075 Martinelli Road
Forestville, CA 95436
800.588.0234
www.hartfordwines.com

Haywood Estate
18000 Gehricke Road
Sonoma, CA 95476
877.996.4299
www.haywoodwinery.com

Hughes Family Vineyards
19201 Sonoma Highway #262
Sonoma, CA 95476
707.575.5222
www.hughesfamilyvineyards.com

Terroirs Artisan Wines
21001 Geyserville Avenue
Geyserville, CA 95441
707.857.4101

Imagery Estate Winery
14335 Sonoma Highway
Glen Ellen, CA 95442
877.550.4278
www.imagerywinery.com

Iron Horse Vineyards
9786 Ross Station Road
Sebastopol, CA 95472
707.887.1507
www.ironhorsevineyards.com

J. Rochioli Vineyard and Winery
6192 Westside Road
Healdsburg, CA 95448
707.433.2305
www.rochioliwinery.com

Jacuzzi Family Vineyards
24724 Arnold Drive
Sonoma, CA 95476
707.931.7575
www.jacuzziwines.com

Jordan Vineyard & Winery
1474 Alexander Valley Road
Healdsburg, CA 95448
800.654.1213
www.jordanwinery.com

Keller Estate Winery & Vineyards
5875 Lakeville Highway
Petaluma, CA 94954
707.765.2117
www.kellerestate.com

Kendall-Jackson Vineyard Estates
5007 Fulton Road
Fulton, CA 95439
707.571.8100
www.kj.com

Lambert Bridge Winery
4085 West Dry Creek Road
Healdsburg, CA 95448
707.431.9600
www.lambertbridge.com

Lancaster Estate
15001 Chalk Hill Road
Healdsburg, CA 95448
707.433.8178
www.lancaster-estate.com

Landmark Label Manufacturing, Inc.
47623 Fremont Boulevard
Fremont, CA 94538
408.262.6111
www.landmarklabel.com

Landmark Vineyards
P.O. Box 340
Kenwood, CA 95452
707.833.0053
www.landmarkwine.com

Ledson Winery & Vineyards
7335 Sonoma Highway
Kenwood, CA 95409
707.537.3810
www.ledson.com

MacMurray Ranch
3387 Dry Creek Road
Healdsburg, CA 95448
888.668.7729
www.macmurrayranch.com

Matanzas Creek Winery
6097 Bennett Valley Road
Santa Rosa, CA 95404
800.590.6464
www.matanzascreek.com

Matrix Winery
3291 Westside Road
Healdsburg, CA 95448
707.433.1911
www.matrixwinery.com

Mazzocco Sonoma Winery
1400 Lytton Springs Road
Healdsburg, CA 95448
707.433.9035
www.mazzocco.com

Michel-Schlumberger Wine Estate
4155 Wine Creek Road
Healdsburg, CA 95448
707.433.7427
www.michelschlumberger.com
www.benchlandblog.com

Papapietro Perry Winery
4791 Dry Creek Road
Healdsburg, CA 95448
707.433.0422
www.papapietro-perry.com

Passalacqua Winery
3805 Lambert Bridge Road
Healdsburg, CA 95448
707.433.5550
www.passalacquawinery.com

Pellegrini Family Vineyards
4055 West Olivet Road
Santa Rosa, CA 95401
650.589.1313
www.pellegrinisonoma.com

Quivira Vineyards
4900 West Dry Creek Road
Healdsburg, CA 95448
707.431.8354
www.quivirawine.com

Robledo Family Winery
21901 Bonness Road
Sonoma, CA 95476
888.939.6903
www.robledofamilywinery.com

Rodney Strong Vineyards
11455 Old Redwood Highway
Healdsburg, CA 95448
707.431.1533
www.rodneystrong.com

Russian Hill Estate Winery
4525 Slusser Road
Windsor, CA 95492
707.575.9428
www.russianhillwinery.com

Sbragia Family Vineyards
9990 Dry Creek Road
Geyserville, CA 95441
707.473.2992
www.sbragia.com

Seghesio Family Vineyards
14730 Grove Street
Healdsburg, CA 95448
707.433.3579
www.seghesio.com

Seguin Moreau Napa Cooperage
151 Camino Dorado
Napa, CA 94558
707.252.3408
www.seguinmoreau.com

Simi Winery
16275 Healdsburg Avenue
St. Helena, CA 95448
800.746.4880
www.simiwinery.com

Sonoma–Cutrer Vineyards
4401 Slusser Road
Windsor, CA 95492
707.528.1181
www.sonomacutrer.com

Stonestreet Winery
7111 Highway 128
Healdsburg, CA 95448
800.355.8008
www.stonestreetwines.com

Stryker Sonoma Winery
5110 Highway 128
Geyserville, CA 95441
707.433.1944
www.strykersonoma.com

Taylor Lombardo Architects
529 Commercial Street, Suite 400
San Francisco, CA 94111
415.433.7777
www.taylorlombardo.com

Vérité Winery
4611 Thomas Road
Healdsburg, CA 95448
800.273.0177
www.veritewines.com

Viansa Italian Village & Winery
25200 Arnold Drive
Sonoma, CA 95476
800.995.4740
www.viansa.com

Wilson Winery
1960 Dry Creek Road
Healdsburg, CA 95448
707.433.4355
www.wilsonwinery.com

THE PANACHE COLLECTION

CREATING SPECTACULAR PUBLICATIONS FOR DISCERNING READERS

Dream Homes Series
An Exclusive Showcase of the Finest Architects, Designers and Builders

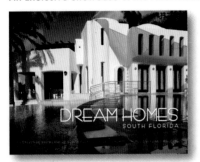

Carolinas
Chicago
Coastal California
Colorado
Deserts
Florida
Georgia
Los Angeles
Metro New York
Michigan
Minnesota
New England
New Jersey

Northern California
Ohio & Pennsylvania
Pacific Northwest
Philadelphia
South Florida
Southwest
Tennessee
Texas
Washington, D.C.

Spectacular Homes Series
An Exclusive Showcase of the Finest Interior Designers

California
Carolinas
Chicago
Colorado
Florida
Georgia
Heartland
London
Michigan
Minnesota
New England

New York
Ohio & Pennsylvania
Pacific Northwest
Philadelphia
South Florida
Southwest
Tennessee
Texas
Toronto
Washington, D.C.
Western Canada

Perspectives on Design Series
Design Philosophies Expressed by Leading Professionals

Carolinas
Chicago
Colorado
Florida
Georgia

Minnesota
New England
Pacific Northwest
Southwest

City by Design Series
An Architectural Perspective

Atlanta
Charlotte
Chicago
Dallas
Denver
Orlando
Phoenix
San Francisco
Texas

Spectacular Wineries Series
A Captivating Tour of Established, Estate and Boutique Wineries

California's Central Coast
Napa Valley
New York
Sonoma County

Art of Celebration Series
The Making of a Gala

New York Style
South Florida Style
Washington, D.C. Style

Specialty Titles

Distinguished Inns of North America
Extraordinary Homes California

Spectacular Golf of Colorado
Spectacular Golf of Texas
Spectacular Hotels

Spectacular Restaurants of Texas
Visions of Design

Panache Partners, LLC   1424 Gables Court   Plano, Texas 75075   469.246.6060   www.panache.com